T.R. Lawrence's enthralling book on shopping the Marrakesh, Morocco souk took me back 20 years. An avid Moroccophile, I spent the 80's goir̶ ̶b̶a̶c̶k̶ and forth to Casablanca enroute to fabled Marrakesh and the ̶c̶o̶u̶n̶t̶r̶y̶ ̶a̶t̶ ̶w̶h̶o̶l̶e̶. Lawrence did the same. He surfed the souk. I was ̶a̶ ̶j̶o̶u̶r̶n̶a̶l̶i̶s̶t̶ ̶ r̶-chant buying rugs, jewelry, textiles, furniture ̶t̶o̶ ̶t̶h̶e̶ ̶U̶S̶ ̶w̶h̶e̶n̶ Morocco was "hot" and still is. Able to r̶ ̶ ̶ ̶ ̶ ̶ ̶ ̶ ̶ ̶ ̶m̶o̶v̶e̶-ment, smells, mystery and magic of the far ̶t̶h̶e̶ three-ring-circus Jemma-el-Fna square, Law̶ ̶ ̶ ̶ ̶ ̶ ̶ ̶ ̶ ̶ ̶ ̶ ̶ ̶ ̶ ̶ ̶t̶ mercan-tilism. It is a great read.

> —Landt Dennis, Author of *Living in ̶M̶orocco: Design from Casablanca to Marrakesh.*

A fun, page-turning travelogue. This was an enjoyable read.

There are at least three reasons why The first is to learn the intricate pathways of the medina in Marrakech. My wife and I were there on a trip about two decades after the author's first trip. Of course, the author got into much more than we did on a casual two-week trip, but I can tell you that it's an authentic reflection of that country.

The second reason to read this novel is because it's a business lesson about how to become an entrepreneur. There are many examples of big corporations and big inventions that were started with a simple idea or a hands-on experiment where one step led to another. In this case, it was a surfing trip turned into something much more.

The third bonus from the book is to understand the underlying idea—really the spirit—that life can be interesting, but you must be fearless enough to travel outside of your comfort zone. For TR Lawrence, one adventure leads to another and before one knows what has happened, an entire life's course has been altered for the better. The elder reader will appreciate the spirit of the past; the younger reader should find it an inspiration.

> —Eric Rudd, Artist/Author of *Sayulita Mariposa Sayulita Butterfly*

This engaging read describes the partly fictionalized Moroccan adventures of T.R. Lawrence, co-owner with his wife, Linda, of a textile emporium known as Nomads of Santa Fe. A young Lawrence, fresh out of college, is seduced by the exotic maelstrom that is the Marrakech medina, where he and his wife would eventually live off and on over the course of 25 years. Amusing flashbacks focus on the mythical Pink City before its "discovery" by the international jet set.

> —Kitty Morse, Author of *Cooking at the Kasbah: Recipes from my Moroccan Kitchen* and *Mint Tea and Minarets: a Banquet of Moroccan memories.*

Reading *Lawrence of Marrakech* I was instantly transported to another time and another place. I imagined myself back in one of my favorite haunts: the Djemma el Fna, replete with its snake charmers, acrobats, fire-eaters and storytellers, as well as the winding alleyways and souks that lie beyond. I cannot but admire Lawrence's sense of adventure, bravery and fun in the 1970s, those more innocent days before the advent of the internet, mobile phones, social media etc. I recommend this book to any lover of Morocco.

–Richard Hamilton, Author of *The Last Storytellers:*
Tales from the Heart of Morocco.

Lawrence of Marrakesh is the story of TR Lawrence's passion for Moroccan textiles and the many adventures to which that passion leads. Set against the sights, the sounds, and the smells of Marrakesh, in all their beauty and rawness, it ranges from the manicured gardens of the luxurious Mamounia Hotel to the dark, narrow alleyways of old town. And of course, there are the busy souks. It is a fascinating story, well told. As you will learn, no one visits the markets of Marrakesh without a guide. Let Lawrence be yours.

–D R Baker, Author of *The Devil's Money*

T.R. Lawrence's colorful account and images of his times spent in Marrakech during an era when tourists were a rarity and importing Moroccan goods was even more rare is captivating, moving, and educational. T.R. brings the reader with him on his journey, from the eye-opening adventures he experiences during his first visit—which was intended to be a casual surf vacation—through the relationships he built there and the successful business that ensued. The inside look at every day Moroccan life coupled with his adventurous, warm, and inquisitive spirit brings the culture of this city in the heart of Morocco to life. He details the warmth and customs of the local setting, along with the quirks of doing business in a far away land that was, at that time, undiscovered.

–Corinne Gaffner Garcia, Managing Editor of *Western Art & Architecture*

An embellished fiction based on the true adventures of a naïve entrepreneur navigating successfully the souks of Marrakech and Moroccan culture and contributing, in no small way, to advancing Moroccan style in America.

–Tim Resch, President, Friends of Morocco

Lawrence
of Marrakech

FROM THE MAGICAL MARKETS OF MOROCCO

BY T. R. LAWRENCE

NOMADS
PUBLISHING

Published by
Nomads Publishing, a division of Nomads of Santa Fe
PO Box 6874
Santa Fe, NM 87502-6874
www.nomadsofsantafe.com

Printed and bound in USA

Library of Congress Control Number: 2019908277

ISBN 978-1-7328976-0-1   Color Paperback
ISBN 978-1-7328976-1-8   B/W Paperback
ISBN 978-1-7328976-2-5   Kindle (Mobi)
ISBN 978-1-7328976-3-2   All other E books (Epub)

Text copyright T. R. Lawrence
Photos copyright T. R. Lawrence and Linda O'Leary unless other wise noted.

Editor: Jeff Braucher
Cover Designer: Leslie Waltzer
Cover Photo: Jeff Debevc
Interior Design: Robert Erlichman
Contributing Artwork: Christopher Mayes
Contributing Photography: David Saxe

Dedication

To my wife and best friend, Linda O'Leary. Without her insight and discipline this novel would never have happened. She has lived this life with me, traveling the world, while working side by side for our joint success. The true love of my life.

I also dedicate this to my parents, Muriel and Chip Lawrence who prepared me for the real world.

The Reason Why

In all my years of having a retail store and telling stories of my Moroccan experiences, people would often say to me that I should write a book. I finally learned to listen.

Disclaimer

This book is a work of fiction, although many of the stories are written exactly as they happened during my years of travel to Morocco. Others have been embellished, using my artistic license. I will let the reader decide which is which.

Note: Our rendition of the Moroccan language, Darija, is phonetic.

Acknowledgements

◇◇◇◇◇◇◇◇◇◇◇◇◇◇◇◇◇◇◇◇◇◇

I wish to thank all my Moroccan friends:

Boujamaa El Khang

Noreddine El Khang

Habib El Khang

Braheim Belguermah

Ben Sheriff at Bazar du Sud, and his four sons. Moulay Sheriff,
Ismael, Moulay Arabi, and Youseff.

Haj El Khanjar

Omar El Khanjar

Elbachir Ettari

Laarabi Abdellatif

Mustapha El Yid

To my Santa Fe group who helped make this happen:

Karen Bomm

Jeff Braucher

Leslie Waltzer

Robert Erlichman

Contents

◇◇◇◇◇◇◇◇◇

T. R. Lawrence & Linda O'Leary
Private Collection

◇◇◇◇◇◇◇◇◇◇◇◇◇◇◇◇◇◇◇◇

After buying thousands of carpets in Morocco, these are what I consider to be the most valuable and collectable. Value to me has to do with tightness of weave, the use of primarily natural dyes, and those that are woven by a skilled weaver. These textiles were also our teachers, and we learned through them to appreciate this quality.

Many of the weavings have been included in Museum shows across the United States, in private exhibitions, and have been photographed in other publications.

See the Collection

You can see the best of the T. R. Lawrence & Linda O'Leary Private Collection from the comfort of your home right through the pages of this book. Using cutting-edge augmented reality technology from RealityX2 explore the fabulous rugs that make up this one-of-a-kind collection. See one you really like–you can even purchase it through the app.

HERE'S HOW

1. Download the free App for iOS or Android
    (You can use the QR code or go to the store.)
2. Open the App on your Smartphone or Tablet
3. Point your camera at the rug on the facing page or the image
    on page 75
4. Enjoy!

Silk and Wool Zemmour Saddle Rug, circa 1900.
One of the weavings for sale from the T. R. Lawrence/Linda O'Leary Private Collection.

Prelude

◇◇◇◇◇◇◇◇◇◇◇◇◇◇◇

A FEW MONTHS before I graduated from college in the spring of 1978, I read an article in the March issue of *Surfing Illustrated* that would change my life forever. I decided to forgo graduate school, pack a bag, and stick out my thumb toward New York's JFK airport. I bought a ticket and boarded a plane, waking up shortly before landing in Marrakech, Morocco.

What started out as a surfing safari ended up being an intriguing business and learning opportunity I never would have dreamed of. I would be challenged, tempted, and seduced by the people, the arts, the colors and smells, in the twisting, narrow alleys of Marrakech. With my beautiful girlfriend and future wife, I would live in the Kasbah on and off for the next twenty-five years, earning the respect of all the merchants, the traders, and their neighbors.

Sensing no fear and rarely feeling lost or threatened, I discovered antiquities hidden for centuries in the markets, treasures buried in the sands of Sahara, and new friends in Djemma el Fna, the Square of the Dead.

Chapter One

Above the Bus Station

◇◇◇◇◇◇◇◇◇◇◇◇◇◇◇◇◇◇◇◇◇◇◇◇◇

"FASTEN YOUR SEATBELTS, we will be landing in the next thirty minutes" came over the airplane's PA system in three different languages: first in Arabic, then French, and finally English. I was a little hung over after drinking at least four sixteen-ounce Schlitz Malt Liquor beers, and was not able to sleep much on the eight-hour flight from New York's JFK. It was the first of June and a few of the passengers told me it was already hot in Marrakech, so be prepared for the hot, dry air coming out of the Sahara Desert.

Marrakech sits on the edge of the desert to the south and is ringed by the Atlas Mountains to the north and the east. The view from the airplane made for a picturesque photograph with palm trees, snow-capped mountains, and barren landscape dotted with white-washed, fortified villages. I almost made out the people riding or leading donkeys through the vast groves of olives, oranges, and figs. It was early morning, around eight o'clock, and the morning fog was coming off the Atlantic Ocean one hundred miles away. As we made our approach, Marrakech looked like an enormous pink oasis sprinkled with green date palms and winding streets that led to dead ends. The runway was lined with old WWII fighter planes left behind by the U.S. Army Air Forces and large white tribal tents with black motifs embroidered on the top and sides. Immigration officials used these tents to process tourist visas and check for contraband entering the country.

I was one of the last passengers leaving the aircraft because I was assigned seat 56K, the last seat on the plane right next to the bathrooms, which became my seat of choice for the next ten years. I grabbed my carry-on luggage, descended the aluminum ramp, and was immediately aware of the heat on my neck like I had eaten some hot Indian spices the day before. Up ahead the Moroccan military carried old Russian Uzis, all wearing cheap Foster Grant sunglasses. Inside the terminal was complete chaos, long lines due to closed checkpoints, and lots of lost luggage, even though this was a direct flight. It seemed like no one really cared, and if you didn't tip them to help you locate it, it could end up in Cairo or Istanbul. Years later I would go searching for my lost luggage, a sewing machine, and some tequila; entering an upstairs warehouse of about 5,000 square feet filled top to bottom with lost, lonely luggage, all rifled with their entire contents thrown about. No one I would ever know or question there at the airport ever knew what happened to the baggage after it left the upstairs warehouse.

Now our luggage seemed to be taking forever to disembark the airplane. The porters hand carried it, with no conveyor belts in sight, and took us through customs. The many custom officials—a bizarre group of men, different sizes, shapes, stripes, and colors—were all wearing loose-fitting faded uniforms with gun holsters but no pistols. I found out later that this was because of the recent assassination attempt on the king, who doesn't trust anyone having a gun, especially the customs officials who typically come from Berber tribal groups. I sensed these officials were just looking for some bribes so they could buy breakfast.

As hot and dry as it was, and with no air-conditioning at the airport, I would have thought I'd be perspiring. Instead, the sweat was evaporating as quickly as it secreted.

I didn't know why, but I was beginning to enjoy this place with its circuslike, laissez-faire attitude and international flavor. I got in line to exchange dollars for dirhams, their Moroccan currency. Long lines, impatient travelers, and suspicious money traders made it quite difficult to exchange money. They seemed to hate traveler's checks, older American hundred-dollar bills, or any currency that had ever been torn or written on. For the money they refused to exchange, they just said, "Go to Gueliz," and I thought, *Where in the hell is that?* I finally exchanged a few hundred dollars and got a large stack of Moroccan dirhams, all with the picture of the king on them. I soon realized that this picture was always on television, on lamp posts, and in every household in Morocco, and that the people always spoke politely of him—or else.

I passed under a sign that said *"Merhabban"*—"welcome" to Marrakech, and saw numerous sand-colored Renaults and Citroens under the shade of a few trees. Most of the people on the flight were ushered onto the many tour buses that would take them around the country and the imperial cities of Fez, Marrakech, and Rabat. But what caught my eye were a few of the horse-drawn carriages just outside the taxi stand.

It appeared that older Moroccans still preferred the ride from the airport in carriages, and it was at this exact moment that a well-dressed stranger said to me, "Good morning, would you like to share a carriage to the old city?" He politely introduced himself as Ben Ali Karbush and motioned for the driver to retrieve my baggage. It was then that the driver recognized him, looked him in the eyes, and kissed his own ring finger.

"La bas" – *"La bas alec"* – *"Colshee la bas"* – *"Hamdula"*: I heard these phrases and would learn them quickly, never to forget them, and used them for the next twenty-five years.

The driver cracked his whip, said *"Peacemela"*—"let God protect us"—and off we went down a dirt road leading away from the airport. All the carriages were painted green and pulled by beautiful well-fed and manicured Arabian horses. I was told later that the men treat their horses better than they treat their women.

As soon as we left the airport parking lot, even though Ben Ali seemed sleepy—it must have been those large brown Moroccan eyes—he began to tell me about himself and his family. He was from a wealthy, famous fifth generation family that resided next to the Mamounia Hotel—so famous that one of the mosques outside of the medina was named after his grandfather, the old Iman of Marrakech.

They had amassed a large fortune, even though the government had changed hands multiple times during this period, because the iman was above the law. They were religious leaders to the king, the Pashas, the Ciads, and all the tribes from the south, and because of this, they could keep their wealth and properties intact. This was how they ended up with a home next to the Mamounia Hotel, with vast olive oil farms, and with businesses in the Kasbah.

He then wanted to know where I had gone to college, what my family did, and asked what I was doing here. I told him I had planned to go surfing in Anchor Point just north of Agadir, had majored in fine arts, and was well traveled as a child, and that my parents now lived in Houston, Texas. The idea of my focusing on the arts interested him, and he said I would love the art in Marrakech. About the surfing, he mentioned it might be extremely dangerous in that area, and to watch out for the people living there. They were from the Rehamna tribe, half Arab and half Berber, and could not be trusted. All the while the carriage driver was listening to our conversation and plotting an additional stop before reaching the home of the Sidi Karbush.

We were now winding through the olive groves, which seemed to grow right up to the walls of the medina. Up ahead I saw a sign in English that said, "Welcome to the Holiday Inn."

The driver turned around on his bench and asked Ben Ali if it would be all right to pick up another passenger who was working at the hotel. She was an employee and a neighbor of his on Riad Zitone. Ben Ali said, "Why not?" and we rode around to the back of the hotel to the employee entrance, where everyone there seemed to know our carriage driver. We stopped under a few orange trees, and the driver disappeared and then reappeared with a brass tray containing a teapot, small tea glasses the color of cobalt blue and decorated with a gold filigree design, a bunch of mint leaves, and a lump of sugar the size of a baseball. He jammed the leaves and the ball of sugar into the teapot, poured a glass of tea into one of the dark blue glasses, and then poured the tea from the glass back into the teapot. It seemed like the ceremony was over, but then he poured the tea back into the glasses from at least a foot above. The glasses were far too hot to hold, so he gave each of us an old aluminum bracelet to put around the small glasses so we could hold them. About thirty minutes had passed since we left the airport, and it was getting a little warmer, so I was thirsty, but I was not prepared for how sweet the tea would be.

Ben Ali was slurping his tea when a young woman appeared wearing all black and a veil. She spoke to the driver, who acknowledged her like an old friend. She didn't sit in the back of the carriage but chose to sit on the bench with the driver. Another crack of the whip and off we went toward the walls of the medina.

The road changed from dirt to gray asphalt as we left the gardens of the Holiday Inn. The woman twisted around and whispered to Ben Ali in the distinct dialect of Berber and Arabic. It was a quick conversation with a lot of hand movements. I waited a moment and then asked Ben Ali what she had said. He replied that she wanted to know where I was from and if I had decided on a hotel in Marrakech. Up to that moment I had no idea; I hadn't even thought about where I would be staying. I just assumed I would wander around and eventually find a room, not knowing it might be more difficult than I had thought. She now spoke to me in broken English and suggested I come with her to the CTM Hotel on the Djemma el Fna, where she would introduce me to her mother, who worked there.

I estimated we were approaching the Mamounia Hotel and the villa of the Karbushes because Ben Ali took a comb from his pocket and began to comb his hair and then straighten his tie. Up ahead were the ramparts of the old medina walls, and around the corner an immense parking lot filled with similar green carriages. I saw the drivers squatting on the ground under orange trees, sipping mint tea, and security officers wearing baggy pants, colorful red or green sashes holding up their trousers, Egyptian white cotton collarless shirts with bright red hats from Fez, and large brass pendants held on big chains around their necks. Beyond the parking lot and the security kiosks I could see the splendor of La Mamounia Hotel, considered by many to be one of the top ten hotels in the world.

Ben Ali recognized one of his friends by the entrance to the hotel and decided to disembark. He took out his business card from his shirt pocket and wrote something on the back, handed it to me, and said he hoped to see me soon, then disappeared among the crowd. I turned the card over and read, "Please be my guest next Friday afternoon after prayers at the poolside of this hotel. Just mention my name to the doorman and he will escort you to the restaurant by the pool."

Now alone in the back of the carriage, I heard the woman give orders to the driver, and we left the Mamounia Hotel quickly and headed toward the Djemma el Fna and the CTM Hotel. At that moment I had no way of knowing that the Djemma el Fna and the CTM Hotel would be my home away from home for the next decade.

As soon as Ben Ali had gone, the woman in the front introduced herself and took off her veil. She said her name was Mariam from the Glaoua tribe near Taroudant, southeast of here, over the mountains. She also told me her mother at the CTM Hotel would assist me with anything I might need.

The street instantly became wider and cleaner, lined with orange and cypress trees. I noticed men with homemade six-foot-long brooms who were sweeping the streets of even the tiniest of particles left over from the night before. I asked Mariam about the tall ancient building to our left, and she replied that it was the Koutoubia Mosque, built in the eleventh century by the Almohad dynasty, and one of the most famous mosques in all of Morocco. This landmark would become my lighthouse, because every time I got lost, I would search the skyline, find the mosque, and adjust my direction.

Up ahead I saw thousands of people milling around, and the driver started yelling, *"Belek! Belek!"*—"watch out!"—and whipped the horse a few more times to get us through the crowds. With such commotion and activity on the square, I just looked straight ahead and decided to suspend my curiosity until later.

We stopped next to a long line of buses in front of the Café de France. I was surrounded by complete havoc—tour buses, baggage carriers, street callers yelling to get more passengers, dozens of shoe shine men, and young tourist guides waiting for the unsuspecting lost tourist. I tried to pay the driver, but he waved me off, indicating that Ben Ali had already paid the fare. Mariam saw her mother standing in the entry of the hotel and motioned me to follow her with my luggage.

In front of the CTM Hotel, across the street from the Djemma el Fna, Mariam introduced me to her mother, Brecka. Brecka was the washerwoman for the entire hotel and worked there every day but Friday. Mariam told me that her mother was once married to a man from the Sahara who had ten wives in his harem. Her mother was the youngest of the wives and had only one child, herself, and when her father died a few years later, the other nine wives got all the possessions and money and left her mother penniless. Brecka had only one other relative, a sister who was a slave in the king's palace and was never able to leave.

Little did I know then that this dark woman named Brecka would be so instrumental in all my activities in Marrakech for many years to come. She would teach me about the Djinn, the black magic of North Africa, and protect me from my ignorance in the medina. Brecka was no more than five feet in height, so dark that she looked purple, and was wearing at least four layers of sequined, gauzy material, cinched with a belt wrapped twice around her tiny waist. I noticed that the skin on her arms resembled the hide of a crocodile, so I decided right then to help her by rubbing some of my Lubriderm lotion on her arms every day after she finished the laundry.

Mariam and Brecka escorted me through the arched wooden door of the hotel, where a super small man introduced himself, then picked up my baggage and dropped it on the tile floor in front of the desk. But I couldn't understand his introduction. Mariam told me he was called La Hassan, "the Dumb," because he had only half a tongue and couldn't hear well.

La Hassan would also become a good friend and protect and follow me around whenever the hotel wasn't busy. Years later, when La Hassan was older and of no further use to the hotel, I spied him in the new part of town, Gueliz, and offered him a ride in my car. I gestured with my hands for him to get in, but La Hassan didn't move. I tried again and just got a mixed emotion, so I got out and grabbed him by the hand and led him to the open passenger door. La Hassan acted frightened, and that was when I realized he had never been in an automobile. We rode around town until I found the restaurant he liked, all the while I could see fear on his face. I handed him enough dirhams to last a few days. He muttered thank you and good-bye. This would be the last time I would ever see La Hassan.

The manager of the hotel appeared, introduced himself as Omar, and began to tell me the sad story that the hotel was "complete," meaning no vacancies, even at this early hour in the morning. Brecka and Mariam inquired about the room in the back of the hotel that the management reserved for people they considered VIPs. "Can he pay a little extra?" I should have realized I could have bargained for the room. Instead I handed him my passport, paid full price for a week, and was informed that I could retrieve my passport in twenty-four hours.

At that moment I noticed Omar had eleven fingers, five on his right hand and six on his left. He saw me looking at his left hand. He told me that he was born in his mother's home, with no doctor present, and that having an extra finger is considered good luck. Omar motioned for La Hassan to take my baggage up to my room. I politely excused myself, saying good-bye to Mariam and Brecka, and followed La Hassan up the stairs. There were two flights of stairs to get to the terrace, and every other step seemed to be cracked or broken. It was OK going up, but I sensed coming down could be dangerous.

Reaching the top of the stairs, I overtook La Hassan and marveled at the rather large, tiled courtyard surrounded by turquoise-painted doors leading to private quarters. Antique urns circled a fountain, some with painted tribal designs, others growing honeysuckle and papyrus. My room was indeed in the far rear of the hotel, but I could still hear the noise of the street, with the buses coming in and out of the depot.

La Hassan set my luggage down in front of my room door, which seemed larger than the others and had an old latch that would not deter a child. The key looked handmade, but the lock could have been sprung easily with a finishing nail.

Entering the room, I quickly realized how tired I was; I hadn't slept much on the plane the night before because of all the anticipation and wonderment of coming to Morocco. I turned around and gave La Hassan a few dirhams and looked around for the first time.

The room had its own bathroom and a window looking out onto an alley instead of the courtyard. I left the door open because the room smelled of Moroccan tobacco and perfume, and my nose picked up another scent coming from the bathroom. I opened the bathroom door to find, instead of a normal toilet, just two cement imprints of shoes straddling a hole in the floor. A faucet came out of the wall on the left side of the hole. Near the toilet hole was a pipe coming again out of the wall but higher up. I determined that this must be the shower, with no faucet head just straight pipe, and that the water flowed down the toilet hole. There were no closets in the room or hangers, just hooks in the walls. The walls were swimming in brown and yellow that could have been painted by Omar with his eleven fingers.

Exhausted, I lay down on the bed, which may have been stuffed with straw or old rags, but it certainly didn't come from a mattress factory. I took a few deep breaths and fell fast asleep until early evening.

Waking up to the loud cries of the hustlers filling the bus, going who knows where, I thought about taking a shower, but I saw no towels and when I turned on the water all I got were some gurgling sounds. I decided to ask Omar what the problem was. I walked toward the stairs, intending to go to the lobby, but noticed another flight of stairs to the rooftop, so instead I went up. They were in better condition but much narrower and steeper. Once on the roof terrace I soon realized I had an unobstructed 360-degree view of the entire city of Marrakech. Directly below was the Djemma el Fna, to my left was the Koutoubia Mosque, to my right a long alleyway I would later learn was Riad Zitone, the street of the olives, and directly ahead the enormous doors to the Kasbah.

I counted my blessings that on my first day I met Mariam and was led to this fascinating hotel, where I would be able to observe the people in the square, the commerce at the bus station, and the customs of this country undisturbed. Now I could hear my stomach making noises like the water pipe in my room, and I looked out across the square to a grouping of black tents with smoke rising out of them. Guessing they might be portable restaurants since they weren't there in the morning when I checked in, I descended the stairs only to run right into Omar looking out the hotel door at all the commotion in the street. Someone on a bicycle had been run over by a donkey cart that had gotten loose from its owner. This accident attracted no less than fifty people all trying to help and offer suggestions. While I was waiting for all this activity to subside, I requested some towels from Omar and asked about the water for the shower. Omar told me he'd make sure the towels would be in my room when I returned, but the availability of water was another matter. The government usually turned off the water to the medina in the daytime, and it only came on late at night, so Omar said I should listen for the water coming up the pipes at night and take a shower then, and he would give me a clean bucket to catch some for flushing the toilet.

The group outside had dispersed without too much shouting and shoving, so I exited the hotel and headed for the tents in the middle of the square. Once outside I realized I was the only one dressed in Western clothes and vowed that tomorrow I would try to find an outfit that resembled the uniform of the doorman at the Mamounia Hotel.

The square had a perpetual floating population of people made up of wild, pale-skin Berbers from the mountain villages, Sub-Saharan blacks from the edge of the desert, and Arab tribes that camped outside the walls of the city. As I approached the restaurants, I felt that the activity was beginning to heat up. Dancing groups, acrobats, scribes, storytellers, snake charmers, and pick-pockets were all positioning themselves for a good spot on the square.

As I neared the outdoor food vendors, a tall, big man with a great smile and a mouth full of gold teeth gestured to me to come over and sample his brochettes of mixed meat. Most of the tents seemed to be serving the same thing, but under the lights of the gas lanterns it was hard to say. So, I entered the tent with the least amount of smoke in it, which just happened to be where the big man with all the gold teeth was. No one in the tent noticed me because they were all eating with their hands, faces down, and concentrating on licking their fingers. I just pointed at what I thought might be good, a small collection of mixed meats on a kebob stick. He pointed to an empty bench and brought over my food on an old metal tray with a few limp French fries thrown in. As I looked around the tent, there was an interesting assortment of dinner guests, but no women or children were present. This would be the first time, but not the last, when I would be without silverware and using only my fingers to eat. Pulling the meat from the metal kebob stick without the help of a fork was difficult—but not as difficult as chewing it. This meat must have been an old goat since it didn't taste like beef.

During this chewing exercise I heard a hissing sound behind my back. I tried to ignore it and went on chewing, but it didn't stop; it just got louder. I finally turned around to see a tall, skinny, brownish young man dressed in clothes of different sizes. While I was turned, I happened to see a small, dark hand reach up from under the table and grab the remaining brochettes on my plate. Before I could even react, he had crawled from under the table and exited between a slit in the tent wall. The hissing continued, so I turned back around to address the young man. He gestured that he would like a cigarette, puffing on the space between his two fingers. The owner of the restaurant had seen the little gypsy child steal my remaining brochettes and motioned to the hissing Moroccan to leave me alone. My first dinner on the square will always remain a memorable meal. I washed it all down with a warm Orangina soda and headed back to the CTM Hotel.

Omar was waiting at the reception desk and handed me the key, along with the towels and bucket he promised, and told me to open the shower faucet so I would hear the water when the city turned it on.

At exactly two a.m. I was awakened by the sound of water bubbling up from underneath the hotel. I jumped out of bed, grabbed the orange plastic bucket, and showered next to the hole in the floor. I was lucky; I filled the bucket and finished rinsing off just as the water ceased to come out of the pipe. The towels Omar gave me all had a strange scent of olive oil, apparently from the olive soap they must have washed them in. I glanced out the window to the alley below and saw a few strange travelers sleeping, squatting with their full-length, hooded *djellabas* thrown over them. What a great first day!

While it was still dark outside, I woke up to the singing of the local *moktar* at the nearby mosque. There was a cool desert breeze coming through the window, and the chanting hypnotized me back to sleep. The next noises I heard came from the bus station—men yelling the names of cities, looking for more customers to fill the empty seats. "Agadir," "Casablanca," "Fez," "Essaouira," were shouted repeatedly, adding even more to the usual confusion on the square, until all available seats were taken.

I quickly dressed in the only other clothes I had besides my airplane outfit. I brushed my teeth with the water from the bucket and used some of the rest to flush the toilet. I latched and locked the primitive door and then climbed up the stairs to the rooftop where I saw that Mariam's mother, Brecka, had already begun to wash yesterday's laundry. I remembered seeing a café next to the hotel and decided to see what kind of breakfast they served. The Café de France was one of the most famous cafés in Marrakech, sitting directly across the street from the square, with one of the best vantage points for people-watching. No one was required to buy anything, so many people just sat there all day, commenting on the passersby and sipping a glass of water. This was also the focal point for the king's secret police because they could observe all the people coming and going at the bus station.

I selected a table close to the sidewalk, quickly realizing my mistake since all the beggars could stick their hands out in my face. There were not just a few but bunches of them, and they seemed to work in teams. One stood making hand motions, pretending to be eating, while the other, with hands out, cupped them for coins. They were a ragtag group, wearing an assortment of clothes of different colors, all stitched together like a clown outfit from a circus. Besides the beggars, numerous other groups stopped at my table: several shoeshine men tapping their brush on the side of their wooden box; young boys selling cigarettes one at a time, jiggling their coins in their hands; small children with dirty faces and hands selling Chiclets; and old men wearing colorful red outfits with tassels on their hats, which looked like Mexican sombreros, selling cups of water out of a goat-skin bag.

One waiter approached, but unsure of what to order, I just pointed to what was at another table nearby. Fresh orange juice, croissants with chocolate inside, and coffee with fresh milk. It took quite a bit of time because of all the customers taking breakfast there who were waiting to meet their friends or starting their day. All the while the steady stream of beggars never let up. I now wished I had a few coins to give them so they would leave me alone. Before my food arrived, I started looking for another table, preferably inside, so I could be left alone, but all the tables were full, and other patrons stood alongside tiled walls waiting for a table to open. So I just stayed put. Then I spotted a waiter with a large tray above his head that looked like the food I had ordered. About the time my food arrived, it seemed that every fly in Marrakech woke up and began buzzing around my head. The orange juice was chilled and served in a tall, clear glass, the coffee with milk in another clear glass but about half the size, and the croissant on a small metal tray—all fresh and delicious.

While I was there, no one got up or moved. It appeared that they had settled in for the day to gossip or hiss at the women walking past the café. But it was the hissing noise coming from behind me that particularly caught my attention. I turned around, now recognizing it as the same sound I heard the night before at the tent restaurant.

"*Sa-bah AlKh-ir*"—which I took for "good morning"—came from a rather tall teenager, lean and dark. He looked like he could have been in a *National Geographic* photograph taken in the Sahara Desert. He had no meat on his bones, rather large hands and feet, and a terrible scar from his wrist to his shoulder, as if someone had poured gasoline on his arm and then set it on fire. Since I put up no resistance, he introduced himself as Ismael and immediately rose from his table and joined me. He caught the eye of one of the waiters who must know him and ordered what I was having.

Ismael told me he was from an old family in Marrakech that had been in the carpet business for decades, but that his father died last year due to poor health. He was now living with his mother and sister. Ismael learned English at night at the American Institute in the new part of town and worked as a guide when he got the chance. I had a thousand questions to ask him but decided to wait awhile until we at least finished our breakfast. The crowd started to thin out as the stores surrounding the square began to open. The waiters now lined the counter looking like penguins in their white shirts and black pants.

Ismael told me that he had known all these waiters since he was a child, and that people in Marrakech never seemed to change jobs once they had one. I was thinking of ordering another coffee with milk when Ismael motioned for the check and asked me if I would like to visit some of Marrakech's historic sites. I was still considering what to answer when the check arrived on a small metal tray, and the waiter just stood at the table waiting to be paid. Out of habit I reviewed the check and saw that everything we ordered was all the same price. Ten dirhams each, or about ten cents for each coffee, juice, and pastry. When I realized I wasn't being charged for Ismael's breakfast, I asked why, and he gestured to me that he would return later to pay. *Enshalah*—God willing. I paid the bill and asked Ismael to ask the waiter if I could get my change in coins so I wouldn't be caught without them by the beggars and street people in the future. I was determined not to let that spoil my holiday.

Ismael thanked his friend the waiter, stood up in a split second, and said, "*Ella imshio*, toot sweet"—"let's go quickly"—"and see the sights of Marrakech before it gets too hot." Up to this point I had totally forgotten about the reason I came to Morocco, which was to go surfing, not necessarily to see the tourist spots. I vowed to ask him later that afternoon about Agadir and the possibility of surfing there.

We circumvented the square, shook off a few beggars and shoeshine men, and headed down a long, twisted alley toward the Bahia Palace. There were few tourists at the palace and only two tour buses. I inquired about it, and Ismael told me that this was not tourist season and that Ramadan was coming in a few weeks. No one wanted to be in Morocco during the fasting period from sunup to sundown. I had read about Ramadan in the Muslim world, so I was familiar with this religious holiday, but didn't understand till then how difficult it must be not to have water during the daylight hours in this heat.

The centuries-old Bahia Palace didn't hold much interest for me, but what did were all the gigantic birds' nests perched on top of the parapet walls of the palace. Even before I could ask him something, Ismael sensed my silent questions and answered them. The nests belonged to a species of large storks that made their home in Marrakech, and it was believed to be very good luck to have one of these nests on top of your home. I suspected that Ismael had been doing these types of quick tours for quite a while. We stood around, kicked up some sand, touched a few old stones, and finally I said, "What's next?" As we were leaving the Bahia Palace, heading south, Ismael pointed out Meelah, the Jewish quarter, and the alley called Riad Zitone, which was a shortcut back to the square.

We continued walking farther from the square on a much wider road with sidewalks. No beggars or shoeshine men here, just commerce—horse-drawn wagons piled to the top with imported merchandise, donkey carts stacked with vegetables of every color, size, and shape, and men carrying live sheep on their shoulders, probably on their way to a slaughterhouse nearby. We continued south from the palace, and it was on a corner with a few cafés and restaurants for local people that I eyed a beer sign hidden behind some metal latticework that said "Stork Beer" with a picture of the same big bird that roosts on the parapets of the palace. It appeared to be a small restaurant with a few tables, and next door was another café with lots of empty tables awaiting customers. I made a mental note of where we were so I could come back in the early evening and have a few of the local beers.

We now turned onto an even busier street with dozens of *mashus* looking for work—men who pushed their own cart, not pulled by animals. They moved the bulk of the merchandise from the outskirts of the city into the medina because in the inner city the streets became alleys and were far too narrow for cars, trucks, or animals. Ismael said we were now headed to the Kasbah, the section of the city where we would find the Saadian tombs. Shop after shop lined the street, each with its own specialty, from selling underwear and socks to brass trays. Many of the shops were extremely small, and the owners would climb up into their above-ground stalls to sell their wares. Only men—all with beards and white skull caps—ran these shops. Ismael asked me to stop gazing at the sites and hurry up, because soon would be the call to prayers and the entrance to the tombs would be closed until later that afternoon.

We entered the tombs through a large arched gateway and viewed the graveyard of some of Morocco's famous kings. It looked a lot like the Bahia Palace, with plaster falling off the walls, weeds growing between the stone floor tiles—a complete lack of maintenance. After just a few minutes I told Ismael I had seen enough and asked if he knew someplace we could have lunch.

Just outside the walls of the Kasbah, Ismael pushed me through two old wooden doors and declared that this restaurant was owned by a *haj*, a holy man, who was a close friend of his father. The place was full of smoke, and I could barely make out the other customers eating there. Ismael inquired about the whereabouts of the owner, and the waiter told him he was at the mosque and should return after prayers. Ismael ordered his favorite, lamb cutlets.

While waiting for the lunch, I observed a scene I would never forget. The same waiter who waited on us gathered up about a dozen metal kebob skewers that had been lying on some dirty plates in the rear of the restaurant. He grabbed a small box of Tide detergent and a bucket of water, then proceeded to the sidewalk. Once there, he dropped the kebob sticks in the cobblestone street, dusted them with a little bit of Tide, then poured some water on them. He rolled them back and forth until he thought they were clean, then rinsed them with the remaining water from the bucket. Picking them up and going back into the restaurant, he opened the door to an ancient refrigerator and began pushing the cubes of meat, the hearts, or the livers onto the sticks, and then put them on the barbeque. All the while I was thinking about getting food poisoning and vowed never to eat kebobs.

The lamb cutlets finally came, served with a round loaf of bread the diameter of a Frisbee and heavy as a brick. I watched the other customers pulling out the center of the fresh dough and leaving it on their plates. Then they jammed the meat into what was left of the loaf to create a Marrakech-style sandwich. After watching how they kept the food and how it was prepared, I longed for some peanut butter. Ismael loved this greasy meat and kept licking his fingers since there were no napkins.

As we were finishing our meal, the owner came back from prayers and offered Ismael and me some warm mineral water named Oulmes, with two small semi-clean glasses. They both spoke for some time, nodding at me occasionally and making numerous hand gestures. Some of the other customers now realized my presence and turned and welcomed me with a smile. Everyone had a beard and wore either a skull cap or turban and loose-fitting clothes with sandals. I now realized how much I must stand out and renewed my vow to buy a Moroccan outfit.

The streets were now completely empty after lunch, so I asked Ismael what was going on. He mentioned that after noon prayers, everyone went home to eat lunch with friends or family. Lunch in Morocco is like the dinner meal in the U.S., he explained, the only difference being that at lunch in Morocco they all eat as much as they possibly can, then fall asleep till they are called back to the mosque to pray, and then return to work. I paid the bill for both of us and left a generous tip. As we were leaving the restaurant, I turned back to see the waiter kissing the tip I left him with a large smile on his twisted face.

With a stomach full of meat and bread, I too thought a small siesta would be appreciated, so I asked Ismael to walk me back to the square and the hotel. He told me we didn't have far to go, and as we turned the corner I again saw the Stork beer sign behind the lattice wall, and I then knew where I was. When we arrived at the hotel, even the square was empty, and the desk man was nowhere to be found, so I just reached across the counter and retrieved my key. The hotel was quiet, the bus station had no callers, so it seemed to be a great time for a nap.

Opening the door to my room, I immediately checked if the water had somehow been turned on during the day, and quickly saw that it hadn't, but I still had some left in the bucket. Outside in the alley two cats were fighting, but the noise didn't stop me from falling fast asleep. I had the same recurring dream. *I am at a beach resort, going into every surf shop looking for the right size and shape surfboard to buy, only to be discouraged because they don't have the right one. Some-*

times I am talking with strangers about where to buy the board, or where to go surfing. Across the street on the beach there is no surf, but on the horizon, I see a monster wave over fifty feet high getting ready to break or close out. The dream continued until I finally woke up to the calls to prayer from the mosque across the street from the square.

I lay around a few minutes, but the continuous onslaught of flies that must have woken up also at the call to prayer made it impossible to relax in bed. These flies were moisture-seeking insects that went for your eyes and lips and never let up. Still no sign of the water being turned on, I decided to buy some bottled water to have in the room just in case. I had been sleeping in my clothes, so I just put on my shoes, grabbed my key and the remaining dirhams, and quickly opened the bedroom door.

I startled a man standing very near the door. Dressed in an old wool djellaba, he looked like he just got off the bus from some desert village. With an orange turban wrapped around his head, a full black beard, and old leather sandals with tire treads for soles, he appeared to be a Berber. Startled though he was, he smiled and muttered, "Merhabban," which I already knew meant "welcome." He wandered off as I locked my door, and I began to wonder what in the hell he was doing standing in front of my door. Then I realized he had been watching me through the large keyhole. How long he had been crouching there peeping, I would never know. It was just another lesson about what to expect in this foreign country.

Outside the hotel, the square was coming to life. The snake charmers were pushing up their umbrellas and the circles were beginning to form as the storytellers started reciting their oral history. I walked toward the ancient post office, knowing I needed to turn down an alley right before I would get there. At the entrance to the alley were a group of nine old men, all wearing sunglasses, standing very straight, and holding wooden bowls or metal cups that they kept moving up and down like they were keeping the beat to some music I couldn't hear. I stopped to watch, then reached into my pocket for some coins. I dropped a five-dirham coin into the wood bowl of the tallest of the blind beggars. Knowing by the sound of the coin being deposited what the amount was, he immediately smiled and said,

"Salaam Alaikum"—"Peace be unto you."

Giving had always made me feel good, and now I could anticipate how good drinking a few cold beers would be.

Traveling down the alley of some twenty small restaurants, I looked through the windows and saw only men hunched over their food, eating with their hands. Apparently, no women or children ate in any of these restaurants. I guessed they were all men from the mountains and not traveling with their families. The fronts of all the restaurants had a refrigerated glass case with different kinds of meat: lamb, goat, cow, camel, chicken, and pigeons, but no pig. Hearts, lungs, livers, kidneys, wings, feet, and eyeballs, but no pork. Most of these restaurants resembled the one where I had lunch, all burning the small, soft, dirty charcoal and serving lots of mint tea. For a moment I thought I was lost, but as I approached a busy street intersection and turned the corner, the familiar Stork beer sign appeared behind the metal latticework.

The entrance was hard to find because of all the plants and palms close to the door. It had the air of being secretive. There were only five tables, with each table having three metal chairs positioned around them. No one else was there, and I selected a table I thought would give me a view of the street so I could watch the action. Once sitting, I realized no table had a view of the street. The tables were hidden, and the reason, I discovered, was that alcohol was forbidden in this part of the city. Passersby would not be able to see the customers who were drinking beer and who might be their neighbors.

A few moments later a short, slim young man with a half-grown mustache and sweat streaming down his face came from downstairs in the back of the restaurant and dropped a menu printed on only one page on my table. He introduced himself as Aziz, from Ourika Valley, and in broken English said he was the waiter, busboy, and cook. I pointed to the Stork beer sign and showed two fingers. He nodded and disappeared. After what seemed like a long time, Aziz re-appeared with two dark-green bottles and a small glass used for mint tea on an old brass tray. The beers were neither hot nor cold, and the bottles smelled a little like old cheese. So I closed my eyes for a second and wondered what the hell I was doing, and then thought that I wouldn't want it any other way. I started planning my adventures for the next day—finding out about Anchor Point and buying an outfit like the doormen wore at the Mamounia Hotel.

After my second beer, Aziz reappeared, and I ordered one more beer and a shrimp omelet with French fries. This, I would come to understand, took considerable time since he had to peel and clean the tiny shrimp. When the food finally arrived, it was delicious—the om-elet was hot and buttery with the small shrimp scattered throughout, and the French fries, fried in olive oil, were fantastic. Aziz brought the bill, which totaled less than seven dollars, and I decided right then that coming every evening to have a few beers and eat a shrimp omelet would become a ritual.

All the time I had been in the restaurant, I was the only custom-er. Aziz stood at the end of the table after bringing the bill, waiting to be paid. I asked him the name of the restaurant and he replied "Iceberg," and I thought, *What an appropriate name for a restaurant with lukewarm beer.* I gave Aziz a two-dollar tip, which he immedi-ately grabbed, bringing the money to his lips and kissing it. A big smile erupted on his face, and he gladly said, "*Shokoran bazeef, insho-fuk*"—"Thank you very much, see you."

As I left the restaurant I saw how dark it had become and how much the traffic had increased—mostly men heading home after work, and mothers and their daughters doing last-minute shopping for meat and vegetables. I decided to take the same way back to the CTM Hotel and leave the adventures for the daylight hours.

Approaching the square I noticed a whole new group of acrobats, each standing almost seven feet tall, wearing long white gowns, and forming pyramids that reached to the sky. They attracted a large crowd of onlookers that applauded every somersault, cartwheel, and gymnastic trick. One of their crew, a man dressed in a snow leopard skin and holding a large straw hat, walked among the people, requesting payments for the performance. Most of the onlookers just looked straight ahead without reaching into their pockets for some coins to drop in the hat. Then the man noticed me watching the acrobats and asked me to contribute.

As I reached into my pocket for some coins, he stepped closer when he realized I was a tourist and whispered in my ear, "Some spices for the mind, my brother?" I had a good idea what he was talking about, so I reached deeper into my pocket until I felt some paper money. I dropped the money into his straw hat and noticed it had only small copper coins in it; the paper money stood out among the coins. The man smiled, then nodded as he reached into his small snakeskin bag around his waist, grasped something inside the pouch, and offered to shake my hand. I immediately felt a small, square object in my right hand. This whole interaction took less than twenty seconds. I put the spices for my mind in the back pocket of my pants, and the leopard skin man disappeared in the crowd, searching for more coins for the performers.

With the small chunk of hashish in my back pocket, I went off in search of a pipe so I could smoke a little before I fell asleep. I wandered through the crowds in the square, fascinated by the sights, smells, and music that pulsated from each small group of guitar players. Near the portable barber shop, I saw a very large dark man sitting cross-legged on a straw mat by a lantern with hundreds of long wooden pipes for sale. Also lying on the mat next to the pipes were a few monkey skulls, a basket of terra-cotta pipe bowls, and an array of AK-47 rifle bullets that had been drilled out to make key chains. I handed out a few coins, not knowing what the pipe cost, but it must have been enough because he threw in a box of wax matches.

Wandering back toward the hotel, I stopped briefly at the Café de France, where I had breakfast that morning, to buy a 7 Up. At the hotel a small group of people were in the lobby checking in. La Hassan recognized me and gave me the key to my room. I asked about the water, but he just said, "Enshalah"—"God willing." Instead of going to my room, I decided to head up to the terrace and observe the square, drink my 7 Up, and smoke a little of the brown square from the leopard-skinned man. Watching the square from the rooftop terrace gave me a completely different viewpoint. I saw in the middle of the square a pile of black tarps. Occasionally the heap would move a little to the right or the left, and then be still for a while. I could only imagine what might be living under the black canvas, so I decided to investigate in the morning.

I could feel the small square of hashish in my pocket, and my mind was begging for a few puffs. No one else was on the terrace to snitch on me, so I just lit up, sat back, and watched the smoke mingle with the barbecue smoke from charcoal fires on the square. I started to think about the surfing at Anchor Point and remembered the pictures of the monstrous waves of the North Atlantic, but for some reason I kept feeling I was being pulled into the magic of the medina of Marrakech.

I had lost complete track of time, probably because of the hashish and having no one to talk to. The hotel was quiet now even with all the rooms full. I had forgotten to drink any of the 7 Up, which was hot by now, but decided to wait a few minutes and use it to brush my teeth since I had no water. I walked back down the stairs, avoiding the broken ones, crossed the terrace and only saw a few lights under the doors of the other travelers. A note was tacked to my door, saying my passport was at the reception desk. I decided it could wait until tomorrow.

I took a sip of the 7 Up and used the rest to brush my teeth. I turned on the ceiling fan, turned down the sheets, and there in the middle of the bed was a rather large brown scorpion. Shocked, I wondered how long it had been there, and being a little stoned, I was lucky I didn't just try to pick it up and throw it out the window. I had never seen a live scorpion or known anyone who had seen one either. So I attempted to kill it with my 7 Up bottle, only to knock it off the bed. When it hit the floor it scurried off, running with its tail straight out, and slithered under my door, headed for the terrace. Having just seen the scorpion, I knew it would be difficult to fall asleep, so I just lay there listening to the sounds of the alley—a great mixture of cats fighting, doors opening and closing, a few infants crying for food. As I waited for the water to be turned on, I eventually fell asleep and dreamed of scorpions crawling up the walls of my hotel room and falling from the ceiling onto my bed.

It was still dark outside when I awoke to the call for prayers. I lay there for a while, trying to fall back asleep, but it was no use. I decided to hurry up and get back to the rooftop terrace to see what had happened to the moveable black tarp. On the rooftop I immediately encountered Mariam's mother, Brecka. She was busy building a wood fire under a large metal cauldron to heat the water so she could wash all the sheets and towels from the hotel. It was still too dark to see my new interest in the square, so I helped Brecka with her chores. She was still wearing the same type of clothes she was wearing a few days before, multilayers of gauzy material all different colors and sequins everywhere. I helped her gather more wood for her fire and started putting the linens in the water. She seemed to appreciate the help but was suspicious of why I was helping her.

The sun was coming up, so I hurried to the wall overlooking the square to see what became of the movable black tarp. Yes, it was still there but had moved about ten feet from where it had been the night before. Brecka was then busy scrubbing the towels on a wooden washboard, oblivious to me watching her.

I noticed that the waiters had started to open the Café de France, putting out the chairs and sweeping last night's cigarette butts into the street. A few donkey carts overloaded to the max were outside, and I saw the open sores where the leather harness rubbed against their shoulders. Many young boys carried large bundles of fresh-cut flowers. I realized it was too early for the beggars and shoeshine men to get up, so it was a great time to eat my breakfast of fresh orange juice, coffee with milk, and a few croissants. I descended the stairs only to be met by Omar, with the eleven fingers, and La Hassan, the Dumb. Omar mentioned that he had my passport to return, and I said I'd pick it up later, "Enshalah," and walked next door to the café.

Soon after entering the café I heard a familiar hiss-hiss, and I knew instantly that it could only be Ismael, the tour guide. He seemed happy to see me and greeted me in the traditional manner: "Good morning, my brother. God is great." He patted the chair next to him, motioning for me to sit down. On the table was a book that appeared well used. Offering it to me, he mentioned that it was an English-Arabic language dictionary that he felt I would get a lot of use out of.

Enjoying the same breakfast as yesterday, I had more time to ask Ismael a multitude of questions, starting with the surf conditions at Anchor Point, and where I could purchase an outfit like I saw the doorman wearing at the Mamounia Hotel. "First things first," he replied. "Let's finish our breakfast because the buses from Agadir have not arrived yet, and the clothing shops in the medina do not open until much later." The beggars and shoeshine men started to show up, but Ismael had selected a table in the back, making it difficult for this group to wander among the tables to beg from us. Also, some of the waiters recognized me and shouted to these people to please leave me alone.

Thirty minutes later we heard the callers crying out, "Agadir! Agadir!"—a city just south of Anchor Point. Knowing the bus was soon to arrive, Ismael and I finished our second coffee, and I asked the waiter to exchange some paper money for some more coins so I would be prepared again for all the poor people I would surely meet that day. We walked into the square to await the bus. Families with their luggage began to form a line. We didn't have to wait long, because in a few minutes a bus coming from Agadir, with all the windows open but all the indoor curtains closed, and its rooftop piled high with baggage, stopped right in front of us. Complete confusion ensued. The passengers attempted to depart the bus at the same time the new passengers were trying to get on. No one seemed upset, so I assumed this must be normal. After the commotion subsided, Ismael went over to the young man who kept yelling "Agadir" even after the bus was full and inquired about the surfing at Anchor Point.

He told Ismael he was familiar with Anchor Point. It was there that the government made iron anchors for ocean-going ships for fifty years, but it had been closed for the last ten years. Concerning surfing, he was only aware that the ocean was calm during the summer months, and that in the winter the ocean was very rough and dangerous for fishing vessels. After Ismael told me this, I realized how naïve I was. Having lived in Hawaii when I was a boy, I never thought about a surfing season; I just assumed there would be waves all year long. My dreams of surfing monstrous waves in the North Atlantic would have to wait.

I now had some serious decisions to make. I grabbed Ismael and headed back to the Café de France to come up with some sort of alternate plan. I still wanted to trade my Western attire for some Moroccan clothes and yellow slippers, and I had yet to set foot in the old bazaar, see the spice market, or visit the Meelah. I told Ismael of my new interests now that my surfing safari was over before it had begun, and then off we went through the square and the arched walls that divided the old city from the new.

❧ Chapter Two ❦

Talking to Me

◇◇◇◇◇◇◇◇◇◇◇◇◇◇◇◇◇◇◇◇◇◇◇◇◇◇◇◇◇◇◇◇◇◇◇◇

ONCE WE WERE INSIDE the walls of the medina, it felt as if time there had stood still, as if we had traveled back to centuries past. It was much more primitive than the rest of Marrakech. Cars were forbidden, and instead it was the bicycles and the donkey carts you had to watch out for, as well as an occasional *carosa*, or mashu cart, being tugged through the alleys by men yelling, "Belek! Belek!"— "watch out!" The alleys were overflowing with every imaginable type of person. We turned down one alley, and to our left I saw thousands of chicken eggs for sale. Next to them, live rabbits and pigeons, and farther on, one old man selling sheep heads with the horns still on them. The eyes of the dead sheep seemed to follow me as I walked past. Up ahead there was a *hammam* (Turkish bath) for the people living in this neighborhood. Ismael told me the baths are for all the men and boys in the morning, and the women and girls in the evening. I suspected that few of the people here had showers or bathtubs in their homes. Since I still didn't have water at my hotel, I wondered how the baths had water during the day. I decided to visit the baths soon to see what they were like.

Continuing on, I saw a few bird cages hanging from a bamboo canopy and a rather large Moroccan man sitting on a small stool in front of his shop. Sticking out of his mouth was one of the long, wooden soup-see pipes that I had bought the other night in the square. I presumed he must be smoking hashish, and as I got nearer he spied me and immediately hid his pipe and small leather pouch under his stool. Ismael apparently knew him and introduced us. He was Boujma from Essaouira, a place I had never heard of. A Portuguese Arab, he specialized in high-quality, one-hundred-percent Egyptian cotton and English felt garments. Boujma slowly opened each cedar trunk with considerable care not to disturb the clothing neatly stacked inside. After seeing most of the caftans, djellabas, capes, and baggy *serwal* pants, I mentioned I would like to be dressed in the same outfit that the doormen of the Mamounia Hotel wore. I was in luck, because it was in this little boutique shop that the corporate owners of the hotel bought the clothes worn by the doormen of that hotel.

I realized Boujma had been trading for many years when he pulled out the exact sizes I needed. I couldn't wait to exchange my American Levi jeans, tennis shoes, and polo shirt and become dressed like a Moroccan. I became interested in buying two white collarless shirts worn outside the pants, one pair of white cotton serwal pants with the baggy crotch and buttons on the ankles. Also, one full-length, V-neck, white *dra* or gown that reached the ground. You had to pull the shirts and dra over your head since there were no buttons or zippers, and the pants had belt loops, but I doubted anyone ever used them.

Having just found exactly what I was looking for, I attempted to find out the prices for all the garments I wanted to purchase. But Boujma would have nothing to do with it until I tried on all the clothes I wanted to buy. He pulled open a heavily embroidered dark drape and stacked all the clothes on another cedar chest in a tiny back room with a large, narrow mirror. I took my time since no one here seemed to be in a hurry. I could hear Ismael and Boujma talking outside in the shop, so I peeked through the curtain and saw them passing the soup-see pipe back and forth. I tried the serwal pants on first, then the collarless shirt. The quality of the cotton was magnificent, and the workmanship superb. Each button was made from mother of pearl and hand sewn. As I looked in the mirror, I sensed how silly I would look to my old friends if they were here now. But they weren't, and this was what I wanted. The pants were extra baggy—I could hide a watermelon in them—and the shirt was beautiful and resembled those worn by Dustin Hoffman and Steve McQueen in the movie *Papillon*. Now the only thing left to finish this outfit was the yellow goat slippers everyone wore.

I pulled back the curtain to show Boujma and Ismael the finished product. Neither say anything, they just smile, and I assumed it was the soup-see that had caught their tongue. Boujma motioned for me to sit on another small stool near the entryway. A small boy emerged from one of the chicken stalls, grabbed a few coins from Boujma's outstretched hand, and hurried off into the crowd to return in a few minutes with a tray of glasses, a bunch of fresh mint leaves, a teapot, and a large lump of sugar. What took place then was the same ritual I had observed outside the Holiday Inn a few days before, except now Boujma took an ornately carved wooden hammer hanging on a silver cord to break up the sugar into midsized chunks and put at least two of them in the teapot.

While Boujma was pouring the tea into the small glasses, an older man wearing very old thick-rimmed glasses walked by selling donuts on a bamboo string. Ismael called the man over and bought one for each of us. The donuts were sweet and tasted of the olive oil they were fried in. We all ate them first because the glasses were too hot to hold. By the time the glasses had cooled off, Boujma reached under his stool and pulled out his secret pouch and filled his soup-see. At first I thought it was hashish, but instead it was something called *kief*, a mixture of tobacco and marijuana. He lit it up, inhaled deeply, waited a few moments, and then exhaled back through the pipe, blowing the ash out of the bowl. He did this a few times, then offered the pipe to Ismael, who followed the same procedure. By the time they offered it to me, I already felt a little high from all the smoke in the shop. I took a little puff and ended up coughing and feeling dizzy. Since I had never been a tobacco smoker, this was not for me.

We each drank three glasses of tea, which was the custom, and then got down to the business of what the clothes cost. I had only been in Marrakech a few days, so my bargaining skills were below zero. I soon realized that Boujma did not bargain at all on his quality and gave me one price for everything. Ismael then began to argue with Boujma about the price, not for me, but for himself and his commission. I would learn later that Boujma hated the street guides and refused to give them any commissions on his sales. Sitting there a little dizzy and high, I decided that I wouldn't need the services of Ismael for the rest of the day and that I could find my own yellow slippers.

Ismael wasn't very happy with me not needing his assistance and left me sitting in the shop with Boujma. I noticed that the man across the alley had been watching me, hoping I would like to buy something from him. Once Ismael was gone, Boujma spoke to me in his broken English. He told me about his life, how he came to Marrakech with a Canadian artist that he lived with in the medina, and where I should go to buy the yellow slippers. Boujma had three cages hanging by chains in the entryway, each with a pair of parakeets in them. I had always believed that people who liked birds were good people, and Boujma was no exception. He opened a few more of his cedar trunks and showed me some of the rare textiles and caftans he had been collecting. The caftans were from the turn of the century and embroidered with gold and silver thread. The textiles were Arabian horse blankets used to adorn the horses after the owners had taken the saddles off. Boujma showed me the cloths of the kings, called *bizouey*, a hand-spun wool so fine you could look right through it.

While I was amusing myself with the fabrics, he reached behind him, brought out a small inlaid bone box, and unlocked it with a small brass key that had been hanging around his neck. Taking something out, he then handed me a black, gooey square of something that smelled of dates and honey. This, Boujma told me, is the famous *marjoun*, a mixture of hash, dates, honey, and spices, which he prepared himself. "Try some this evening and see what happens," he said. I had the feeling that this offering was a sign for me to get going; I had been having such fun I had forgotten about the time. I heard the call to prayers, so it must have been around one o'clock.

Boujma locked the box and placed it in its secret spot behind the drape. He stood up to retrieve my outfit and folded each piece neatly, putting them in white construction paper. While I thanked Boujma for all his help and kindness, a young man walked by selling postcards and jiggling coins in his left hand. He sensed I might be his next customer, so he stopped and showed me the postcards. What caught my interest were the pictures of the snake charmers in

Djemma el Fna. I bought five cards to send to friends and family and figured that if I was ever lost I could just show the snake charmer card and people would point me in the right direction.

Now having no fear of getting lost, I left Boujma with his soup-see, his parakeets, his marjoun, and turned the corner away from chicken alley, only to find myself on an even narrower alley with hundreds of hands turned upward praying for coins. It appeared that at every entrance old men and women slept or sat on dirty cardboard waiting for God to help them. Some of the hands reached out to touch me, and a few of the old beggars tried to block my way, but I just walked faster.

I could see an opening farther down the alley and headed straight for it. When I reached the opening, a fish market was on my right, with various types of fish and eels and mounds of tiny shrimp. The seafood was not displayed on ice, just ancient marble slabs. Unbeknown to me I had just entered the historic spice market of Marrakech. More than fifty stalls sold every exotic spice or remedy from around the world in colorful containers or large burlap bags. I attracted little interest since everyone there was busy buying or selling.

In the middle of the market were tribal women sitting on the ground, some under umbrellas, selling every type of basket imaginable, and another group of women off to the side, all with veils and dressed entirely in black, selling what looked like skull caps. No baseball hats here, nor T-shirts either. I decided one of the hats would help make my outfit more authentic, so I selected a woman sitting by herself with her back leaning against a vacant stall. It was hard to determine her age since she was totally covered and I could only see her brown eyes. If she smiled when she saw me coming, I didn't know, but she immediately started sorting through her inventory of skull caps to find my size. Up to then I didn't know that Americans had such large heads. None of the hats I liked fit till she found one and began to stretch it. After a few pulls and tugs, she deposited it on my head and held up two fingers, indicating the price. A handmade cap for less than a dollar. I was really beginning to love this place.

Out of the corner of my eye I saw a large arched doorway with carpets hanging around it and more carpets hanging on the wall of the rooftops, which led me to believe that this must be the carpet market or bazaar. I decided to wait until tomorrow to explore it and again set off to find my yellow slippers.

I passed through a few more arched entrances and found myself on a wide boulevard heading deeper into the *souk*, market. The street then turned into two much smaller alleys, and at that point I had to make my first decision on which way to go. I was caught up in a wave of people heading somewhere, so I just decided to go with the flow. The right fork was crowded with shops selling fabric and all types of zippers, and the left appeared to have shops with brass and metal trays and assortments of tea glasses. I just guessed and headed to the left, being pushed by the crowd. In this area I didn't notice any tourists or Western influence. One shop after the other were all selling similar items. I believed it must be the logic of safety in numbers.

Up ahead was the donut seller, with a gigantic metal cauldron filled with olive oil, dropping in hunks of fresh dough. He then picked them out of the hot oil with a metal hook and threaded them on a bamboo string. People were lined up to buy the donuts, or just to smell the fresh dough cooking. Next to him was an old man selling hard-boiled sheep eyes, and another selling pomegranates and oranges.

As I continued, the streets became even narrower with mini alleys intersecting them. In one of these alleys I got my first glimpse of the yellow slippers. There must have been at least thirty small shops all next to or across from one another, each with yellow, red, and brown slippers hanging from the ceiling or on small tables in the street. Each shop was elevated higher than street level, and you had to climb up to enter it. Once the merchants noticed me, they all started holding up their slippers and begging me to buy something from them.

At a turn in the alley I saw an older man with a yellow turban and a long white beard—the only merchant who was praying and paying no attention to me. He had many pairs of the yellow slippers, some with leather soles, some with rubber, but only a few made with the used tire treads—the type I liked the most. When he had finished praying, I pointed to a pair sitting on a multicolored cushion, and he just shook his head, held them up, and pointed to my feet, indicating that the shoes were too small. I forgot that Americans have big feet as well as big heads. Like the skull caps that didn't fit me, it might be a challenge to find slippers that were the right size.

He called out to a small boy who was working nearby, told him something, and sent him on his way. Within minutes the boy returned carrying a pair of yellow slippers with soles made with Goodyear treads.

My attempt at buying the yellow slippers had created a lot of activity, and now there were many onlookers all trying to be of some help. Everyone seemed to be arguing with each other over the quality of the shoes, or where they were made. One man in the audience who spoke some English introduced himself and told me he had worked on an American military base outside of town. He also said he greatly respected this older gentleman selling the shoes since he was a holy man, a *haj*, who had made the pilgrimage to Mecca. I asked him how much these types of shoes cost, and he told me thirty-five dirhams, but because they were the largest size available, they would cost forty dirhams. I handed the old man the money. He quickly counted it and then kissed the last bill, and said, "God be with you."

The man who helped me buy the shoes was now quickly becoming the new Ismael, asking me if I wanted to go to the rug market or buy some old brass trays, or needed help with anything. I was beginning to find out that there were hundreds of these unofficial guides in Marrakech, and that they were hard to shake off. Being polite didn't seem to work, and not communicating brought disappointing results, so I would just let them hang around. When they saw I wasn't interested in buying anything, they just drifted off. Staying at the CTM Hotel helped, because Americans never stayed there but at the larger hotels with swimming pools, mainly in Guilez. I didn't get his name, and I'm sure he was just as happy getting the few extra dirhams on the shoe sale.

I now heard the afternoon prayers and was beginning to feel a little lost. I was certain I could backtrack my way out of the souk, but I preferred to try my postcard trick. All the shoppers started to head home after the prayers, and the small alleys were becoming deserted. I was standing in an area where the shoe market ended and the leather bag business began. Latticework suspended by old chains blocked out all sunlight. If I thought there were a lot of shoe stalls, there were twice as many leather bag stores, all about the same size and with a few very old Singer sewing machines, which still appeared to work. Only young boys were in the stalls since the older men had gone to the mosque to pray. I held up my postcard of the snake charmer at the square and gave a lost look. Two of the older boys pointed a finger in the opposite direction I had come from and said something in Arabic, which perhaps meant "good luck."

I started walking in that direction only to realize there were no stores or guides anymore. I was leaving the shopping area of the medina and had wandered into a residential area of ancient homes with green tiled roofs that I later learned was called Bab el Khemis, or streets of the baths. A few doors closed ahead as they saw me, a foreigner, approaching in their neighborhood. I could smell all the aromas of lunches being prepared, and none of them did I recognize.

I just kept walking with my yellow shoes under my arm and carrying my new outfit from Boujma. At one intersection I became a little disoriented because in the middle of the street, which was no more than a wide alley, was a large brass post with old chains attached to hooks in the adobe walls, preventing all traffic except pedestrians. Again I reached into my pocket to fetch my postcard, and at that moment a group of school children come along and politely pointed me in the right direction. I thought I might be getting closer to the square, but little did I know I still had a way to go. This must have been the roundabout way back to the square and the hotel. When I did finally emerge from the souk, I found myself on a busy four-lane street, with thousands of people, mostly men, heading for the Koutoubia Mosque.

Everyone was dressed in flowing white gowns, like the dra I had just purchased from Boujma a few hours before. Outside of the mosque the men and boys were all washing their feet in a fountain directly in front of the magnificent carved doors signaling the entrance. I felt a little out of place watching them, and many of the men were giving me dirty looks so I hastened my pace.

Just around the corner from the mosque I could see the Djemma el Fna and the Café de France, so my postcard trick paid off. I even remembered how to get to the Iceberg Café, so I headed that way to drink a few semi-cold beers and eat a shrimp omelet.

Aziz was downstairs when I arrived. He welcomed me back, and without my ordering or seeing a menu, he served me two beers at once, and the omelet came later.

I left the Iceberg just when it was beginning to get dark outside, so I decided to walk back to the CTM Hotel another way. I had walked at least five miles through the medina and didn't get lost thanks to my postcard. This time, instead of turning left out of the restaurant and walking down past the post office alley, I confidently turned right and passed the small, dirty Shell gas station with only two functional pumps and one attendant. One of the pumps was being operated by hand, so a long line of customers waited to fill up their motorbikes.

Directly across the street from the gas station was a city garden, now completely dark with no street lamps, only shadows of people squatting on the ground with the strong smell of hashish in the air. I wandered among the squatters and found myself staring at the police station—a scary place with its cold stone entrance, thick, heavy steel doors, and steel windows. I heard sounds of men crying coming from the upstairs windows, and I guessed that this was where the police did their interrogations.

I was now beginning to feel that the Marrakech medina was speaking to me—from the morning sounds of the street hustlers shouting under my window, the muezzin's calling the faithful to the mosque, the shoeshine men tapping their wooden boxes looking for customers, and the constant neighing and braying of the horses and donkeys; to the afternoon sounds of the blind beggars chanting the Koran, the snake charmers playing their flutes, and the fresh mint tea being poured into small opaque glasses.

I was still standing there when out of the dark came a wild-looking man with a full beard and Rasta-type hair who stopped in the middle of the street, challenging the few cars that drove by and making these unbelievable animal noises. Across the street sat an older man playing his homemade fiddle, waiting for an appreciative audience. I was unsure what to make of all these noises and sounds of the day that felt directed to me, yet at the same time I sensed that they all seemed to be saying, "Merhabban—welcome—stay to help us, and we will help you."

Crossing the square in the evening was always terribly exciting. I now recognized a few of the entertainers and vendors. What caught my interest tonight was a restaurateur selling fresh snails. He was a big man standing in a cloud of steam, pushing the snails around in a gigantic cauldron. He had drawn a rather large crowd of people, some eating with their fingers, some with toothpicks, and others just witnessing the brave swallow the slime. Next to him a newly formed circle of young men listened to an old man give medical remedies while holding a large glass jar under a lantern. On closer examination I realized that these were leeches sucking to the sides of the glass jar, and then was amazed that they also covered his arms from his elbows to his wrists. I knew that bloodletting had been an ancient remedy for curing anything that might afflict the sick, but this was the twentieth century and Marrakech was living in the past. Most of the onlookers, with their tattered clothing and long sunburnt faces, didn't look like they lived here but from the mountain regions. They all appeared captivated by the leeches and the knowledge of the older gentleman. I began to lose interest and headed across the square to my hotel.

Entering the lobby, I heard La Hassan whistling an unrecognizable tune, and Omar, spying me in the doorway, immediately held up a letter for me with his six-fingered hand. "Your friend Ben Ali Karbush left this here for you and asked me to make sure you receive this message." "*Shokoran bazeef*, thank you, Omar," I replied as I grabbed the letter and then climbed the stairs to the terrace and my room. I located my key nestled next to the postcard in my pocket, opened the heavy nail-studded door, and collapsed on the bed. I reached over to the bureau to retrieve my loo-keys (wax matches) and recovered my soup-see and hashish that I had hidden in my pillow. I lit up, took a long-drawn-out puff, and heard the water starting to gurgle up the pipes in the bathroom. Time to take a quick shower to get the Sahara dust off my body; the letter could wait until tomorrow. Enshalah.

I woke to the first sounds of the muezzin singing the songs of the Koran. After a few minutes I fell back asleep only to be disturbed again by the singing. I looked down at the alley. Still dark out, I could discern a little light on the horizon. I suddenly remembered the letter from Ben Ali. Breaking open the wax seal, I read the message written on elegant stationery. "T.R. Lawrence, you are invited for lunch at our home adjacent to the Mamounia Hotel this coming Friday. We would like you to consider arriving thirty minutes before one o'clock, as my father has some important matters that he would like to discuss with you. Sincerely, your Brother, Ben Ali Karbush." I realized now that the lunch I had been invited to had changed from a meal with Ben Ali at the hotel pool restaurant to something far more interesting. Since today was only Wednesday, I had one more day before the luncheon and decided to go back to the medina and explore the rug souk I had seen yesterday. I held off wearing my new clothes till tomorrow's lunch.

⇗ Chapter Three ⇖

Buy from a Poor Man

⬦⬦⬦⬦⬦⬦⬦⬦⬦⬦⬦⬦⬦⬦⬦⬦⬦⬦⬦⬦

I HAD MY USUAL BREAKFAST and found my way past Boujma's store and turned the corner into what I now called "beggars
alley"—shoulder to shoulder with the crowd and the beggars, who
were now easy to recognize and kept their favorite little sweet spots or
crevices like drug dealers. Up ahead I found the archway to the spice
market, where I noticed the veiled woman who I bought the hat from
yesterday, her eyes smiling at me, and she said, "La bes." I turned and
entered the arches to the carpet bazaar, holding my breath and my
wallet. The colors, patterns, textures, seemed to be exploding and
pulling me farther in. Like something out of an old Oriental painting from North Africa, many merchants were lying around on rugs,
heads propped up by their hands with elbows resting on the floor.

While I was looking around in wonder, realizing my fine arts degree from college did not prepare me for this, I heard something, but
it wasn't the normal Moroccan hiss; it was a plea in English, "Could
you please buy something from a poor man?" "Enshalah," I replied,
and he then mentioned that he had been praying for many years to
meet someone like me, and maybe his prayers had now been answered. He appeared to be about my age, dressed in a traditional
djellaba, with yellow slippers and two skull caps and one baseball
cap cocked sideways. Located near him was a white plastic travel bag
with the Canadian maple leaf imprinted on the side. This Canadian

bag would be with him for the next twenty years, carrying all the medical supplies that he thought were necessary, from cough syrups and nasal sprays to assorted pills of different sizes and shapes. All, I found out later, were prescribed by the medina doctors who gave you only what they thought you could afford, which often had nothing to do with your health—like giving hemorrhoid medicine for a staph infection, or penicillin for arthritis.

"Where did you get that Canadian bag," I asked my new friend. He replied that he had to travel all the way to Vancouver to chase down a man who had written him a bad check on merchandise he had sold him last year, and that he had just returned.

"What happened to the Canadian man?"

"Well, he went bankrupt and could not pay me."

"Why?"

"Well, he could not sell all the leather wallets that I sold him."

"Why not?"

"Well, that's a long story."

"Please tell me. I have time, and let us have tea."

After the tea arrived, and the ceremony of pouring it was completed, my new friend, whose name I didn't know yet, told me he had sold the Canadian man five hundred wallets and put only the best ones on the top of the shipment, with the others that were old or poorly made underneath.

"So you cheated him?" I asked.

"Of course, that is just the way business is done in Marrakech."

For the next twenty years—our relationship lasted that long—I would remind him that this was the reason the man couldn't pay him. This story made a lasting impression on me, and I learned to check everything twice. I now asked him his name, and he replied, "Ahmed, but everyone calls me Parisian because I was raised by a French woman when I was young. My father died at an early age." "So should I call you Parisian?" He responded, "Why not? Everyone else does."

He ushered me into his small showroom where he had beautiful saffron-colored rugs on the floor and interesting camel trappings, but what caught my eye was the small stack of dark red weavings with sequins behind his desk, similar to what I had seen from Boujma's cedar trunks the day before. The desk looked like it had been pirated from the French military decades ago, and I noticed an old black Bell & Howell dial telephone on his desk that probably hadn't worked in years. The Parisian saw me looking at the textiles behind the desk and couldn't wait to show them to me one at a time. All ten pieces appeared to be similar in size, and yet some had exquisite border work and occasionally their design or motif changed completely from one area of the rug to the other. I asked Parisian why, and he said the weaver might have died and someone else had to finish it. I wasn't sure which one I liked the most—all of them called out to me, as if saying, "Please buy me and take me to America where I will be loved and treasured like an orphan child."

Parisian told me the price was one hundred U.S. dollars each, but that I must buy all ten for that price. I said, "Let's have more tea." By our third glass I had already expressed an interest in buying all of them, yet how could I do it? I only had $500 left, having brought enough cash to Morocco for what I thought was just going to be a surfing safari. I then remembered I could get some more cash at the American Express office, so I said to Parisian, "Enshalah, I will be back in a few days."

I woke up early the next morning in anticipation of the luncheon at the Karbush home. I walked upstairs to the rooftop where Brecka was already lighting her fire to heat the water and wash all the sheets and towels. She asked me if I would be attending the lunch at the Karbush home. I told her, "Of course," but wondered how she knew about the invitation. I said I would be back to help her hang the laundry after breakfast at the Café de France. Downstairs in the lobby La Hassan also asked me if I was planning on attending the lunch with Ben Ali.

Outside the hotel door, I bumped into the crazy one-armed woman who was always hanging around the hotel looking for money. She grabbed me with her good arm in a steel grip, and I was unable to get away. It was only after my friend and guide, Ismael, stepped in and pulled her off me that I could manage to break free.

I thanked Ismael for his assistance, and then we sat at our usual table and ordered the *kawa halib* (coffee with steamed milk), pastry, and fresh orange juice. I had become addicted to it. After we had finished our juice, Ismael asked if I was planning to go to the Karbush riad for lunch. "Of course," I replied, "I have been looking forward to this ever since I met Ben Ali at the airport." I stopped eating my pastry and asked him how he knew where I was going. He only smiled without saying a word, and I then realized that Omar had opened my letter, read the contents, told everyone, and then masterfully resealed the envelope. Ismael then said to me, "Lawrence, please do not eat with your left hand during the lunch. I will be waiting to hear all about it when you return."

When I was back upstairs helping Brecka hang the laundry, she told me not to quickly sit in the chair appointed to me but to slowly pick my own. "Why, Brecka?" "Lawrence, it is because of our history of poisoning foreigners and each other." She then reached into her laundry basket and handed me a small bundle of herbs tied up with a multicolored ribbon. Brecka said, "Keep this in your right pocket, and do not tell anyone that you have it." She then proceeded to tell me that this would protect me from the Djinn, which could be in his home. "Thank you, Brecka, I will remember your advice and keep the herbs in my pocket all day, but now let's finish the laundry." Hanging all the sheets and towels normally took an hour, but this morning it was taking much longer since Brecka kept muttering to herself and then looking directly at me. Even so, the time went by quickly, and I excused myself, walked downstairs to my room,

and began to dress in the outfit I had purchased from Boujma. As I looked in the mirror hanging on the inside of the door, I thought, *Wow, what a transformation!* The clothes looked great and I felt like royalty wearing the yellow slippers.

Downstairs the hotel staff was lined up to greet me, all giving suggestions. The name Karbush provoked fear and curiosity at the same time. It must have been because they were extremely wealthy and close friends to the king. I told them all I would remember their advice, and uttered *"Peacemela"*—"God protect me"—as I exited the front door of the hotel.

Luckily, the one-armed woman had moved on, but Ismael was still at the café, nursing his coffee. He got up, wished me good luck, and told me there was something exciting about to happen in my life. "See you later, Ismael," I whispered over my shoulder and set off for the Karbush home via the Koutoubia gardens. Walking through the gardens, I couldn't help but see and smell all the people that were either standing up or squatting down, peeing near the mosque. I guessed this was taken for granted since I hadn't seen any portable toilets or public restrooms. I shook my head, thinking that here was their sacred mosque from the eleventh century and everyone was urinating and defecating near it like they were in a bathroom at an airport.

As I approached the Karbush home, at least twenty different makes and models of cars were in their parking lot. Most of the drivers were wearing black suits and standing around smoking Casa Sport cigarettes and sharing stories. I had no idea that this lunch would involve so many people. The chauffeurs stared at me superstitiously as I walked directly toward the outside gate. I stood there, wondering whether to knock or wait, when a small door indistinguishable from the larger gate opened, and an older man, who gave me the impression that he had worked for the family for years, beckoned me in.

Now standing in the outer garden, I could smell the roses growing everywhere. It didn't take long before Ben Ali came out to greet me, and he took my hand and led me down a grassy path with long, narrow fish ponds on either side. Up ahead was a beautifully carved wooden door, hidden by papyrus growing out of one of the ponds.

Up until then, no one had said anything to me, and while still holding my hand, Ben Ali stopped and said, "Lawrence, how are you? How do you like my city?"

"I'm fantastic, and I'm nuts about Marrakech. I hope my clothes will not offend your father."

"Just the opposite, Lawrence. My father will love seeing an American dressed in his Marrakech finest. He will probably know where you purchased them. Welcome, and follow me, please."

I walked slowly behind him and then entered an extraordinary room that I guessed was his father's office but looked like an art gallery. There were many collections of ancient pottery from Fez and Sali, rare muskets on the walls, and incredible tribal rugs adorning the tiled floors. Looking up I admired the carved and heavily inlaid ceiling beams and the painted plaster work. Ben Ali noticed my admiration and told me his father was a great collector of Moroccan textiles and artifacts and had donated numerous items to the museums of both Marrakech and Casablanca. What caught my interest were small, heavily sequined silk tapestries, so I asked Ben Ali what they were used for and where they came from. "Lawrence, they are antique Berber tribal horse blankets that come from the villages around Khemisset in the Middle Atlas Mountain region. My father never sells or donates these because they were given as gifts. Also, Lawrence, you may see another one today because Haj Sherriff is joining us for lunch, and he knows how much my father prizes them."

From behind me I heard someone clear his throat, so I looked over my shoulder to see a good-looking man, well dressed in a tailored suit, with large rough hands holding a book. Before I could say anything, Ben Ali stepped forward and kissed his father's ring finger, then stepped back and introduced me. "Father, this is the man I met at the airport, Mr. T. R. Lawrence from Houston, Texas." Ahmed Karbush extended his hand and gave me a firm handshake. It was then that I saw he was carrying a copy of *Seven Pillars of Wisdom* by T. E. Lawrence, also known as Lawrence of Arabia. Ahmed Karbush gestured me to take a seat directly across the table from him, and then asked if I had any relation to T. E. Lawrence.

"Not that I know of, but my father's name is A. E. Lawrence Jr., and he was also a military commander from the academy who also happened to greatly resemble T. E. Lawrence in looks and stature."

Ahmed Karbush seemed pleased by my answer and then began to ask a multitude of questions: Where did I go to school? What did I study? Was I well-traveled? What jobs had I had? And he even asked me if I had a girlfriend. I replied to all his questions, remembering that Ben Ali had done the same in the carriage, and Ahmed just sat there and nodded like he already knew the answers. Maybe I had already been investigated, but it was too early to tell.

"Lawrence, I have only a few more questions to ask you, because I am only curious. Do you have any fears, and where, may I ask, did you buy your clothes?" I told him I had grown up on the beaches in Hawaii and had been surfing since I was eleven years old. Surfing is an individual sport and quite dangerous, and since I had started so young, I never learned fear and did not believe in failure. To the other question, I told him about meeting Boujma in the medina and how he had helped me pick out the wardrobe. Ahmed then said he knew Boujma personally and that he liked my truthfulness about my concept of fear.

"Enough for now, let's go join the others," Ahmed said. Exiting the same door he had come in through, we entered a small elevator that took us to the next floor. If I thought his office was extraordinary, this oversized room was magnificent, decorated with treasures from around the world. There must have been over thirty men sitting at a gigantic wooden table, all dressed differently. Some were in hooded djellabas that made them look like members of the Ku Klux Klan, while others were dressed in Western suits without ties, and a few wore vests with baggy pants like mine and yellow shoes, with fez hats perched on their heads.

As Ahmed Karbush began to greet the assembled men, a big, powerful Sub-Saharan black man stepped out from the shadows and positioned himself directly behind him. He had a large jeweled silver dagger draped across his chest, and possibly a handgun strapped to his waist. Mr. Karbush directed me to a chair, and remembering Brecka's advice I moved three chairs to the left instead. Ahmed raised an eyebrow, smiled knowingly, and turned to greet his guests. I perceived that all the men there were businessmen as they stood and formed a line directly in front of their host. I asked Ben Ali, who had sat down next to me, "Who are these men?"

"Lawrence, they are all successful *ciads*—tribal leaders—and governors from different districts in Morocco and have come to pay my father tribute and the money they owe him. Also, many come here to ask for numerous favors in helping to settle disputes between themselves and different tribes."

Each man in turn paused in front of their host, who gave them his blessing while extending his ringed finger for them to kiss. But men who appeared to be of lesser prominence just looked him in the eye and kissed their own hand. This procession seemed to go on forever; meanwhile the house servants were quickly distributing small, sweet cookies and pouring mint tea in dozens of small glasses. After everyone was seated, a peculiar appetizer was served. What looked like eyeballs turned out to be just that—pickled sheep eyes. They just sat there on a large enameled plate looking at me, so I politely refused them and many of the other dishes that seemed too exotic to swallow. No one really cared, including my host, since all were busy filling their stomachs and licking their fingers.

By the time the couscous and lemon chicken arrived, I had become proficient in using my right hand to roll up a small ball of food and then pop it into my mouth. I didn't count how many courses were served, but I was sure they must have presented every delicacy the country had to offer. When the large baskets of figs and other fruit were put on the table, I knew the spectacular lunch was almost over.

Some of the men immediately stood up and exited through another hidden door, presumably leading down to the garden outside. I asked Ben Ali, "Where are all those men going?"

"Lawrence, they are headed to gather up their gifts and reimbursements that they have brought with them. They will pay any debts that they owe us, or for any favors."

Outside in the garden it could have been Christmas in Marrakech. Tied to a thick date palm tree stood a young black stallion scuffing the earth with his hooves, and next to him a beautiful, mature ram. There were large stacks of pile carpets in many colors and designs, drums of olive oil and argan oil, along with coffers of different sizes that I presumed were filled with money. Thrown over a primitive, carved wooden bench was one of the small sequined horse blankets from Khemisset, and standing nearby was Haj Sherriff, who I had spoken to at lunch.

Overlooking all these items and watching everything was the powerful black man, standing with his arms crossed and now wearing a yellow saffron turban.

Finally, Ahmed Karbush arrived in his garden accompanied by a smaller man carrying a calculator. He motioned me over to him. "Lawrence, go over to the Mamounia Hotel with Ben Ali and look around. My business here should take no longer than an hour, and then come back here. I have something to discuss with you." "Of course," I replied. He then called Ben Ali over and told him to take me through another hidden door that led directly to the pool side of the hotel. I looked back and noticed that the man with the calculator had now set up a table in the garden, ledger and pen in hand, and was beginning to record the money and gifts that had been offered.

I followed Ben Ali around a corner, past a large inlaid tile fountain, and walked behind the fountain to yet another door, heavily locked and bolted. Ben Ali took a monster-size key from his djellaba and unlatched the door. For a moment I thought the door wouldn't open, but Ben Ali put his shoulder to it and it sprang open to reveal the beauty of the swimming pool at the hotel.

All around the pool were women sunbathing topless, with few men among them. In the center of the pool was a small island with a palm tree growing out of it. I turned to see Ben Ali with his hands raised up to his eyes to obscure the vision of the topless women. "Lawrence, let's go inside, it is too hot for me here."

I followed Ben Ali around the pool, looking at all the beautiful people. All the guests appeared to be tourists, and I doubted that they ever went into the souks to be challenged by the beggars or the guides. Certainly, I thought, none had ever encountered the one-armed woman.

The poolside bar looked like they would have plenty of ice and cold Heinekens on hand. I ordered a glass of ice and one Heineken to be delivered to our table, which was hidden from the view of the pool. Ben Ali ordered a Sidi Ali water and some smoked almonds and peanuts.

Everyone knew him, and Ben Ali told me that when he was younger, they always used the pool in the summer months, and that the king had installed the door when he built the home for his grand-father.

Years ago I had seen this hotel highlighted on a TV show. They had rated the Mamounia as one of the fifth greatest hotels in the world. After being there only a short time, I would not think other-wise. And after all the lukewarm beers at the Iceberg, this Heineken was fantastic. Realizing how much I was cherishing this ice-cold bev-erage, Ben Ali sat silently till I had finished at least one half of the beer. I dropped a small ice cube in my mouth, and Ben Ali spoke. "Lawrence, my father is very interested in you. He is known to see special traits in people he has just met. I think he is going to ask you for a favor, which he is willing to compensate you for. Relax awhile, I will order you another beer. Would you like something else?"

Perfectly satisfied, I could not imagine needing anything more, so I declined the additional beer and instead just sucked on the ice and ate the almonds. For the next thirty minutes we discussed the fighting in the southern part of the Sahara. The struggle between Morocco and the Polisario was over the Spanish Sahara. The Polisario was a group made up of Algerians, Malis, and Sub-Saharan nomadic inhabitants of Western Sahara. Before my trip I had read about this desert war and the Green March in which the king had promised the Moroccan people who wanted to move south, free land and compen-sation if they would inhabit the area. Ben Ali told me that the army was doing poorly and that the Polisario was approaching Marrakech but still on the other side of the Atlas Mountains.

It was a beautiful afternoon in Marrakech, and time passed quickly.

Without ever getting the check, Ben Ali stood up and motioned for me to follow. As we headed toward the hidden doorway, I glanced over my left shoulder for one last peek at the topless, tanned wom-en, with their bright white bathrobes thrown over turquoise lounge chairs. I told myself that someday I too would be lounging poolside, drinking ice-cold Heinekens.

All the guests were gone, and the gifts put away. I found myself interested in the favor Karbush was about to discuss. Entering the inner office, we came upon Mr. Karbush dusting off a few of his new acquisitions. When he saw us, he dismissed his son, and now we were standing together alone. He began to tell me about Moroccan history. After a short lecture on Moroccan-French relations, he suspected that I was more interested in the antique vase I saw him dusting. He changed his strategy and began to tell me about his passion for collecting Moroccan antiques. The pottery pieces were from the middle of the eighteenth century from an area called Tamarout, near the Algerian border.

Ahmed Karbush then told me that as a child he became interested in the artifacts of the Atlas Mountains, and that his father always had a surprise from that region to give him on his birthday. Now, many years later, he had culled his collection, selling off or donating the duplicates and the pieces that no longer spoke to him. He picked up each piece and cradled it like it was a young child. While watching him, I was becoming more and more fascinated by the antiquities he was showing me, and he could sense my growing passion.

Ahmed then asked me to sit across from him on one of the many leather ottomans to the right of his inlaid ivory and carved ebony wood desk. "Lawrence, I have been watching you, and you appear to think like me and have a great sense of intuition and art appreciation as I do. To change the subject, I would have asked Ben Ali to help you in your education and appreciation of Moroccan Berber art, but he does not know the bazaars in the medina. For this task I have asked my uncle Moktar to assist you and escort you to friends and dealers that could help you in your newfound interest. Do you have any plans for this afternoon?"

"No," I replied, "just my usual late afternoon omelet in the Iceberg restaurant in the medina."

"Good, so you can get started right away. My uncle has been living here for some time, and he enjoys seeing the merchants that he will introduce you to. I also wish to ask you a favor that I will compensate you for, which you might then choose to spend on my friends' merchandise."

Karbush continued, "As you might already know, I have two sons, Ben Ali, who you know, and his brother, Ismael, who is studying in Houston, Texas. He is very different from Ben Ali, and Ismael would like to become a college professor so he never gets his hands dirty. He continues to ask for money, so I have been thinking that you might be able to help me with this. Previously you mentioned that your parents lived in Houston, Texas, and that you were planning to visit them after your trip to Morocco. I would like you to take with you, as a favor to me, $8,000 for Ismael, and for this I will give you $500. It is not a problem internationally, as in the U.S. you need not declare that amount. Is this arrangement satisfactory to you?"

I nodded my head in agreement, and Ahmed then said, "Fine, what day do you plan to leave Marrakech?"

"Enshalah, my flight leaves Casablanca this coming Wednesday."

"My uncle Moktar will take you to Casablanca and will put you in the Colbert Hotel that evening and then assist you in getting to Mohammed V airport the next day."

With this matter finished, Mr. Karbush described each merchant he was going to have Moktar introduce me to. "Many of the dealers I used to know have passed away, and these are their sons, who are about your age and have great respect and knowledge of the arts, although they all seem to be a bit greedy for success." I smiled at that, and he continued.

"Behind the Djemma el Fna is a fonduk called Bab Fath. This is a historic compound for trading and lodging and has been a great secret for many years. A man who has a small shop there is named Bashir, who is a Saharan with all the metal and silver trinkets from that area, and also is known for his rare gun and rifle collection. Another dealer in Bab Fath is Ben Hodge, whose father was a famous collector, mainly of fine Berber tribal jewelry. Ben Hodge has continued to deal in amber, coral, and antique silver pieces.

"The second spot where Moktar will take you is in the oldest part of the medina named Massine, near the street of the ancient baths. A merchant family there has always dealt in fine amber, coral, Tuareg, and Berber pieces, and yet it is the son, Yousef, who has become famous for his collections, which are always for sale. His collections range from the antique green pottery you so admire, to Tuareg leather pieces and other things that come his way. You will enjoy him. He is very educated and modern, also with a home on the beach in Azila, living the good Moroccan dream.

"My fourth recommendation is Haj Medi and his son, Abdulhey, in the Berber rug auction. Haj Medi was the man who first introduced me to the fine horse blankets from Khemisset. The son is also well educated and has a passion for fine textiles, and his father is told to be the one who changed the rug market. It is rumored that for many years Haj Medi hired famous fortune tellers and mystics to travel to the High Atlas and sub-Sahara areas. These fortune tellers and such would be paid for their services in jewelry or weavings since there was no actual paper money or coins being used there. The son is charming and will like you, and the Medi family are great sources for the arts. Abdulhey will also help to educate your eye."

As if on cue, Uncle Moktar arrived in a beautiful blue djellaba and fez hat. With our outfits we made an interesting pair. The shops will now just be reopening after the fourth call to prayer of the day. Ahmed Karbush said to me, "I would like to see you again on Monday afternoon."

Moktar, who had been standing silently by the wall, approached and took my hand, leading me out another door that was closest to the parking lot. Bab Fath fonduk was not far from the Karbush home, so instead of taking a short taxi ride, Moktar and I decided to walk. As we crossed the street he let go of my hand and smiled. I continued to walk beside him, and behind the square, he led me through a narrow, arched opening in an ancient adobe wall. A short tunnel passageway was lined with old doors and windows, and there must have been a bathroom nearby because my nose picked up the odor. Moktar grabbed my elbow and directed me up a flight of stairs leading to many shops surrounding an open courtyard. He pointed out both Bashir and Ben Hodge, who were busy since the market had just reopened.

It was all so biblical, no modern anything, everyone in traditional clothing that had been around for centuries, and experiencing this was like watching *The Ten Commandments* with Charlton Heston as Moses. I promised myself that I would never forget the impression this spectacle had made on me. It was the buying and selling that really captivated me. The marketplace was alive with business, with primitive, rare, unusual artifacts piled on top of one another.

Seeing that Bashir and Ben Hodge were so busy, Moktar walked me back downstairs, held my hand again, and took me through the arched opening in the fonduk. We turned right and entered another arched opening, but this street was more like a tunnel, covered above with woven mats to block out the sun. The street was extremely active with mashus, donkey wagons, and many small butcher shops with meat and entrails hanging on old aluminum meat hooks, and well-lit with bare light bulbs hanging from the ceiling. Many women in veils pulled children alongside them. I seemed to be an amusement to these small children, and I was beginning to think they rarely saw someone like me here in the medina.

Moktar had begun to walk more slowly, and just when I thought we might need to sit down for a while, he pointed out Yousef's business up ahead at a busy intersection where there was a T in the road, directly across the street from the Moussin Mosque. The entrance was simple with glass display cases on either side of the door. "Peacemela," Moktar muttered as we entered the gallery, still holding my hand as if I were blind. A young man was sitting at an inlaid desk, much like the one in Ahmed Karbush's office, and when he recognized Moktar, he jumped up from his seat and leaped for the door to find someone to bring tea for himself and his new guests. The next twenty minutes were spent with Yousef and Moktar laughing, shaking hands, and speaking rapidly in Arabic. This was a stroke of good luck because it allowed me to wander around the gallery and inspect his collections.

While we were there a few men came in toting bags with relics I presumed were for sale. The incense Yousef was burning, the jewelry, the artifacts, and the green, glazed pottery were starting to have a profound effect on me. Why, I wondered, had I never seen a photograph or a magazine article or a news special on these incredible artifacts in this part of the world. Surely I was not the first to stumble on this amazing market of treasures.

I heard a whisper as someone entered the main door. Yousef knew this man and called him over. He was carrying a woven satchel and was dressed differently from the Marrakech people I had seen so far. He appeared to be wrapped in blankets and wore a yellow turban and a big dagger. Moktar also recognized the man, having met him earlier with Ahmed Karbush. I wondered what was in the satchel, and he brought out something wrapped in an old silk scarf. Yousef took hold of the object and unveiled an exquisite brass Russian samovar—a thing of beauty. Both Yousef and Moktar wanted to find out where it was from, what family owned it, and if there was more to their estate. The seller told them the family was from Rabat, worked for the king, and had a few more important pieces but didn't want to sell them now.

The way Moktar and Yousef were caressing the samovar, I knew that the man was not leaving without selling this piece to Yousef, perhaps with Ahmed Karbush's financial help. More glasses of tea, nodding, and a handshake cemented the deal. I never saw any money transfer hands, and guessed it would be forthcoming when the piece sold. Yousef was jubilant; he told Moktar he already had a buyer at the boutique in the Mamounia Hotel. I found all this fascinating. But now Yousef, with his new treasure, had no need for either Moktar or me, so he just pleasantly said to me, "Nice to meet you," and stood to give Moktar a small kiss on each cheek.

Moktar grabbed my hand again and led me out the door and into the street, where now there was a mass of people going somewhere. Moktar told me to stay close since the next steps involved many winding, narrow streets like a spider web of alleys. We wandered through the small dye market, and looking up we saw multicolored yarns hanging on long bamboo poles, all drying in the sun.

Shoulder to shoulder with people in the alleys, I was unable to see much of what lay ahead. Most of the merchants knew or recognized Moktar and asked him to come into their shops. I was certain it was because of me that they wanted to talk to him. He just kept saying *Mushtone baseef* —"we are very busy." We finally arrived at the Berber rug market, which I was familiar with, but we had arrived from a different direction, so I was a bit confused. An auction was about to start, and there were many men in the middle of the small square who appeared to be mostly Berbers from the mountains. I happened to notice the man who had just sold the samovar to Yousef. He must have also had a few carpets to sell from the family in Rabat. Moktar navigated me around the groups of men and headed in the direction of a shop where an older man and his son were waving at us. *This must be Haj Medi and his son*, I thought, and presumed that Ahmed Karbush had called ahead and told them we were coming.

I had already been to the rug bazaar, but only to Parisian's shop, and had not been invited into any of the other stores. Haj Medi's store was close to the Parisian's, so I looked around and noticed him sitting outside on a small stool, watching me being introduced to the Medis. Haj Medi was a short, chubby, very dark man with bright blue eyes. His son introduced himself and his father to me in perfect English. It was apparent that they had known Moktar for a long time.

The son, Abdulhey, looked striking with his wild, kinky black hair and large blue eyes like his father's. Someone was already starting to pour tea as we sat on large poufs waiting for the auction to begin. Abdulhey asked a few questions about myself. I told him I had developed a great affection for the small saddle rugs from Khemisset that I had seen in Mr. Karbush's collection.

The evening's auction began, and there appeared to be a large assortment of carpets and kilims. While the runners were showing their wares and throwing them at Haj Medi's feet, his son was busily explaining to me their origin and approximate age, describing in detail the designs and patterns and what they meant. Many of the designs had to do with the evil eye and protection. Most of these rugs were used as bedding, so the people wanted certain patterns to protect them while they were sleeping. As I remembered Brecka's bundle of mysterious herbs that were still in my right pocket, it all seemed to make a great deal of sense to me.

Rug after rug was shown to Haj Medi, who was bidding on some while others were left in a pile by his feet. The carpets were waiting for the owners to appear and either accept or reject the last bid of the auction. All this while Abdulhey kept telling me about each carpet,

and occasionally called a runner over so he could inspect a weaving and place a bid on the piece. I could easily detect that Abdulhey had great affection for this business, and that his father trusted him on his decisions.

During a break in the auction, Abdulhey offered me more tea and then departed, only to return in a few minutes with a textile rolled up under his arm. He unrolled it on another larger carpet to protect it from getting dirty on the street. Seeing my eyes light up and hearing "Wow!" come out of my mouth, he asked, "Lawrence, is this the quality that you have seen at the Karbush collection?"

I replied, "This is more exquisite than any I have seen before." Abdulhey explained that it was made with wool and silk, dyed with cochineal insect dye, and covered in small silver sequins. He then told me it was not for sale at any price. I touched it and could only imagine the history that went with it, wishing I could buy it.

As the auction was winding down, no more rugs were offered for sale, and the dealers and runners began leaving by the many small alleys that exited the market. All the time I was speaking with Abdulhey, I had completely forgotten about Moktar. He seemed to be having a good time talking with Haj and some of his friends. He then turned to me and asked, "Lawrence, can you find your way back?" "Yes, Moktar, I know the way. Thank you so much for your help today." Moktar left, and then Abdulhey invited me to lunch the next day at their family home on a farm outside of town on the way to Ourika Valley. He said he would send over his father's driver to the CTM Hotel to pick me up. After they locked the doors to their store, Abdulhey extended his hand and said he really enjoyed meeting me and was looking forward to our lunch tomorrow.

Now standing alone, I glanced over my right shoulder to see Parisian still sitting there, nervously twitching and obviously hoping to speak with me. I walked over to where he sat, and he said he had observed me looking at the small sequined saddle rug with great lust and wished to remind me of the ones he had for sale. He mentioned it was getting late and he must go to the mosque before he went home, but told me to come tomorrow. "Enshalah," I replied, and then left by a different alley, where cages of rabbits and pigeons were for sale.

As I returned to the CTM Hotel, I was almost high, as if on hashish, by the things I had seen and the people I had met this day. I once again felt that the Moroccan medina was speaking to me and that I was one of them.

It had begun to get dark, so there were far fewer beggars, but the ones left were aggressive, thrusting out their dirty palms in my face every few steps. One or two began to follow me, but up ahead they saw a few medina policemen and quickly disappeared. I wandered the square for a bit, but then decided to go up to my room for a quick soup-see before heading out for my regular shrimp omelet.

As I entered the Iceberg restaurant, Aziz appeared to have been waiting for me, and without my ordering, he immediately brought me two Stork beers and a small glass. When the shrimp omelet arrived, it looked like I was getting a few more shrimp in it, perhaps because I had been leaving a generous tip. After dinner Aziz told me he would like to invite me to his home in Ourika Valley on his next day off to see his village. Knowing I was running out of time, with less than a week left to my vacation, I politely declined. "Maybe next time, Enshalah," and with that he disappeared and returned with some fresh flan for desert, on the house. It seemed I was making friends wherever I went. What a great city.

Instead of wandering the square I returned to the hotel, knowing that tomorrow was going to be another interesting day with the two o'clock lunch at the Medi farm. No one in the lobby noticed me, so I took my key and headed to my room. Taking a few more puffs of my soup-see, I fell asleep in my clothes while listening to the music on the square.

I was beginning to get used to waking up early. I woke to the first calls to prayer, but then fell back into a light sleep before the muezzin called believers again to the mosque. I decided to get up and went downstairs to be the first customer at the Café de France. Ordering my usual breakfast, I once again observed the early morning ritual of the city waking up. I now sat far back in the café to avoid the early morning beggars. It was too early for Ismael, so when I finished I went to my room and changed into a pair of shorts to help Brecka with the laundry.

Brecka could not wait to ask me about my lunch at the Karbushes. We barely said "La bes" before she asked if I had kept the bundle of herbs in my pocket and changed seats. "Yes, Brecka, I remembered all that you told me." She then continued to question me about the food that was served, how many people were there, followed by an unusual question concerning the host: "Did he seem like a kind man?" I replied, "Yes, Brecka, and the other people there all seemed to like and respect him." Brecka appeared to like that answer, and we got busy doing the laundry.

Once we were finished, I went down to the lobby, where Omar and La Hassan were waiting to hear about my luncheon. I told them I had a fabulous time and had also been inside the Mamounia Hotel and seen the hotel pool with its island and a palm tree growing in the middle. They didn't believe me, so I had to explain it again and again.

Looking out the hotel door, I could see Ismael outside the café. I went to speak with him, thinking he was going to question me about what happened at the luncheon, but instead he said nothing and I was the one to bring it up. I told him about seeing all the guests and the gifts and fabulous artifacts that Ahmed Karbush had collected, and then how Mr. Karbush had his uncle Moktar take me to some shops around town and meet his favorite dealers. At this news Ismael seemed to get upset, although he tried not to show it, but his face tightened into a strange grimace. I continued speaking of other things, the way the men were dressed, the sheep eyeballs for lunch, and all my other observances from the day. Ismael asked what I had planned for today, and I decided not to mention Haj Medi and just said I was planning a quiet day on the terrace, perhaps reading my book.

I went back upstairs to the rooftop terrace, read my book for a few hours, and feeling hungry, started to peer over the wall down to the square, looking for Haj Medi's driver. I looked forward to speaking with Abdulhey and learning more about the saddle rugs from Khemisset. Soon La Hassan walked up the stairs to tell me a man had been sitting in the lobby for quite some time waiting for me. I rushed back to my room and changed from my washing outfit into my V-neck dra. I also grabbed a kilo of sugar that Brecka had brought me, telling me to offer this as a house gift, as this was customary.

Downstairs, sitting on some old cushions that badly needed repair, was a short, skinny man with terrible teeth wearing an old suit that was way too large for him. He introduced himself as Haj Medi's driver and said he was also from Ourika Valley and had the nickname of "Weasel" because of his thin mustache. The car was parked in the parking lot underneath the hotel. Weasel wanted me to sit in the back, but I preferred to sit up front in the passenger seat. We circled the square while Weasel waved to a few of his friends, and then he turned up the music, drove toward the mountains, and looking straight ahead, never said another word.

Our drive did not take long. The mountains were in full view as we turned off the blacktop road to a cobblestone entryway with a large carved wooden gate maintained by another worker of the family. The entire family except Abdulhey was standing in the courtyard, wearing their fiesta best. Haj Medi's wife stood next to him. She was very beautiful and also heavily tattooed, and I could now see where

Abdulhey got his striking features. About twelve people not counting Haj and his wife all waited to greet me. As soon as they each shook my hand, they disappeared like an early morning fog.

Haj grabbed my hand and led me into a magnificent riad, or courtyard, with an impressive variety of flowers and fruit trees in full bloom. Hearing our voices, Abdulhey appeared in his most Western clothes: Levi's, white sneakers, and a polo shirt. He could have been me at the airport. Haj motioned for Abdulhey to take me upstairs on the terrace to see the view.

Spectacular. The mountains seemed so close; the olive and apricot orchards appeared to go on forever. They had an old Range Rover that I suspected was used to drive into the mountains, and a corral of beautiful black Arabian horses, with their trainers, all walking around the stables. Out of curiosity I asked Abdulhey about the small white tent that was on the corner of the terrace. "Lawrence, this is where I prefer to sleep. I feel it must be in my blood to live in a tent."

Abdulhey heard someone signaling for lunch, so we descended the stairs to a monstrous room off the courtyard. The room was full of many more people than those who had met me when I arrived. I shook hands with all of them, smiling and saying, "La bes," and realized there were no women or girls at this gathering. Only men, either relatives or local neighbors, had been invited to see the young American. I felt quite honored. Abdulhey sat next to me at one of the four round low tables, and the small stools we sat on all had tribal cushions.

Just as soon as we were seated, the food started coming. First there was a salad, one that would remain one of my favorites all the years I was in Morocco: shredded ice-cold carrots, mixed with fresh orange juice. Then large platters of lamb, followed by lemon chicken, were placed in the center of the table. Someone, either on my right or left, would reach over, grab a morsel for themselves, or place it on my plate. We all ate with our hands; the only small utensil had been for the carrot salad. When the mounds of couscous and steamed vegetables arrived, I knew how to make the small-size balls, as I had done at Karbush's home, and pop them in my mouth. Round, heavy loaves of bread were placed on all the tables for us to soak up any of the juices.

While we were eating, no one spoke or made any kind of sound, unless to clap hands for a young servant girl to come and clear the plates, or to make a "pus pus" sound that was used to summon more tea to be poured. The guests all continued eating like they were starving refugees, while gulping down glass after glass of Coca-Cola, orange soda, or Olmes mineral water, which was supposed to help with digesting this wide variety of food. After the main dishes, cookies and sweets were served, along with multiple trays of sliced oranges, apples, melons, and fresh strawberries, all from Haj Midi's farm, as Abdulhey proudly told me.

Just as we were finishing, we heard the call to prayer, and everyone excused themselves. Even Abdulhey left. I observed through the doorway all the men busily washing their hands and feet in the fountains in the middle of the courtyard, and then they mysteriously disappeared. I knew they had gone to pray somewhere, so I assumed it must be the garden.

I was left alone in this large room with beautiful carved wooden trunks that adorned all four walls. All the trunks were fastened with ornate handmade locks, except one. And that was the one that kept summoning me. I remembered Ahmed Karbush's story about Haj Medi sending the fortune tellers into the mountains and could sense that these trunks all held exquisite treasures.

I contemplated only a few minutes before I got up and opened the trunk that had been speaking to me. Once I opened the warped lid, it turned out to contain everything and more than I had been expecting: bracelets, necklaces, rings, earrings, and huge silver bracelets that I presumed were ankle adornments—not just a few, but hundreds of items, just thrown in with no apparent order. Some were made with coral, amber, red glass, and precious stones too many to remember. But one piece, a bracelet, stood out from the rest. It was silver, with beautiful fine engraving, and it fit me just right. I had always wanted an old silver bracelet, and this one could have been it. It looked wonderful against my now tan wrist. I can't say I wasn't tempted, because I was, but I somehow began to think this was just a test to see if I was honest. I put the bracelet back among the hundreds of other ones, closed the lid, and returned to my stool.

A few minutes later all the men began returning to the room. Haj Medi led the group, with his son following. Haj walked over to me, gazed directly into my eyes, sizing me up, and looked me up and down. All this time he never said a word, and then he smiled. I realized then that if I had taken the bracelet, this Berber man with his bright blue eyes and dark skin would have known, and any future relationship we might have had would be different.

All the other guests now began to leave, and Haj told me to stay. He opened a few more of the trunks with a bundle of keys that was hanging from a leather cord around his neck. The trunks all had similar items to the one I had opened, and all were filled to the top with antique Berber jewelry. Using his son as an interpreter, he asked me if I knew how to sell any of this jewelry. I simply said, "Enshalah."

Haj then told Abdulhey to show me the collection of horse blankets he had collected. A few they had traded with or purchased from Karbush. The name Karbush went a long way with this family, and somehow they thought I was more successful than I was. But they did discover one thing about me. They had tempted me with all this jewelry, which I could have concealed easily, and I had passed the test.

We drank a few more glasses of mint tea, and then Haj left to lie down and rest. Abdulhey called over to Weasel to take me back to the CTM. We shook hands, and both of us expressed our hope that we would see each other again. Weasel drove me back to town a different way, which was even more picturesque. I was sure that either Haj or Abdulhey had told him to take this route so I could see more of the countryside.

Weasel dropped me off just as the square was about to come back to life. I decided to take a short nap and wake up with the evening call to prayer. I changed out of my white Boujma outfit and put my U.S. street clothes back on, but now with my yellow shoes because my sneakers had gotten so smelly. Even though Brecka and I had washed them, we couldn't get rid of the stench of the street smells, which somehow permeated the rubber.

I ate some fresh fish at stall 57, where my friend with the gold teeth was, and then went back to my room to finish off my hash. It was too early for bed, so I went back downstairs to the square in search of the Gnawa musicians from the south. They moved their position on the square from one day to another, and tonight I found them in the middle. They were playing their three-string guitars, clacking their castanets, and swirling the tassels on their red fez hats, round and round. They played until they appeared to get into some sort of trance, and then just kept on chanting and playing. For a few dirhams, although it wasn't mandatory, you could sit among them and chant too. After a short while, and perhaps because of the hashish, I sat down and began chanting and moving my head back and forth also. I don't know how long I sat there with them, but the square was beginning to thin out when I left to go back to the hotel.

The water was just coming on when I entered my room, so I took the longest shower I had had since I arrived. Tonight I finally felt clean, and then right about the time I was beginning to fall asleep I heard a man's voice yelling in the alley under my window. It appeared he was just screaming to himself, or some unseen person hidden by the shadows, and this went on for some time. I was tempted to yell down at him, or throw some water from my bucket, but decided that might make this nuisance worse. After one hour he just stopped. Maybe he lost his voice, maybe the imaginary or unseen people he was shouting at had disappeared, or maybe whatever cause that justified his yelling had lost its importance.

Morning again came early, with the usual call to prayer, and I was up, eating at Café de France, helping Brecka, and then walking to meet Ahmed Karbush. As I headed up the driveway to the Karbush home, I could see that again there were many cars, with their drivers just standing around, looking bored and hot.

One of the Karbush doorkeepers recognized me, opened the door, and led me into a room I had not seen before—a library lined floor to ceiling with book cases, and featuring plush leather couches and reading lamps on every inlaid table. I was left alone for some time, so I perused his collection of books on Moroccan textiles. Another volume that attracted me was a photography book by a Frenchman named Pierre Bertrand filled with fabulous photographs of Berber men and women in their traditional dress. I found a scrap of paper and a pen and wrote down the information I needed to try to buy my own copy of this book.

I must have sat there for over two hours, and just as I was getting anxious the door opened and Ahmed Karbush appeared, dressed rather sportily. He apologized for the delay, saying, "It's been a busy day with lots of responsibilities," and then asked me if I had been enjoying the Bertrand book I was holding. "His book is incredible, Ahmed, and I hope I can find a copy for my own library." At that moment another door opened, and his servant entered holding an envelope, which he gave to Ahmed. He slowly opened the envelope and counted out $8,000 in all new, crisp hundred-dollar bills, stacked them neatly, and slipped them back into the envelope, which he then handed to me. As I put that envelope in my pants pocket, he counted out five more hundred-dollar bills, put it in another envelope, and shook my hand as he gave it to me. I stood up and put the envelope in my money belt around my waist.

I thanked him for the opportunity to help him, and for allowing Moktar to introduce me to the exceptional merchants. I told him a little of my meeting with Haj Medi and going to his farm. Ahmed asked what I planned to buy with the $500 commission. I said I was going to add $500 more and purchase a few of the small saddle rugs from Khemisset. Ahmed smiled warmly. "Lawrence, that is exactly what I thought you would do."

Ahmed then said he would have Uncle Moktar pick me up at the CTM Hotel in two days after prayers, about 3:00 p.m., to drive me the four hours to Casablanca. Ahmed had already made arrangements for me to stay at the Colbert Hotel that evening. Early the next morning Moktar would take me to the airport for my flight. He stood up, shook my hand again, and then kissed me on both cheeks, smiled, and said, "We will meet again, Enshalah." I thanked Ahmed for his trust in me and told him that within a week his son would have his money.

I followed him out a door to the garden, then to the driveway. Walking back to the CTM Hotel, I reflected again on my holiday. Who would have imagined anything like this happening to a young college graduate on vacation who had only planned to go surfing! I paused for a moment and shoved the $8,000 further down my pants pocket, noticing how good the money felt against my skin.

I made my way back to the rug souk. Now I knew the different entrances to the market and easily found my way to Parisian's shop. He seemed not to have moved since the day before, and took me into his small shop where once again he unfolded each one of the ten Khemisset saddle rugs. He treated them like gold, creating an air of value and intrigue for my purchase. He knew I wanted to buy them and mentioned again that the price was one hundred dollars each, but only if I bought all ten. "I understand, Parisian, and I have come prepared." I took out the commission from my money belt, plus my own money that I had saved for this purchase. I counted it out slowly and kissed the last bill before I placed it in his hand, as I had seen so many of the waiters do.

Parisian smiled at this gesture and rolled all ten of them up into a tight bundle. I then realized I had nothing with me to put them in for the trip home. Parisian understood my problem, left for a few minutes, and returned with an old, used army duffle bag. It was precisely the right size, and with its discreet look I knew it would be perfect for my hitchhiking experience from JFK when I returned.

The shops were beginning to close, so I grabbed my duffle bag, threw it over my shoulder, and said, "Shokoran bazeef, my brother," and headed back to the CTM Hotel.

Once upstairs in my room I inspected each rug again. The room was now covered with small weavings thrown over the bed, the door frame, and almost out the window. I decided then that Brecka and I would clean these weavings tomorrow to kill any bugs that might have infested them in the souk.

I stacked them in a small pile, lit up a little of the hashish I had left, and looked out on the alley with a full moon in the distance. For a moment I reflected again on the initial reason why I traveled to Morocco—to surf the North Atlantic. Little did I know when I first arrived what lay ahead and what treasures I would find.

Morning came early, but I was beginning to like it, and I knew today would be a busy day. I walked downstairs and over to the Café de France, finding Ismael at our usual table. "Where have you been, Lawrence, and have you bought anything recently?" I told him of my

David Saxe, Photographer

Silk and Wool Zemmour Saddle Rug, circa 1900.
One of the weavings for sale from the T. R. Lawrence/Linda O'Leary Private Collection.

INSTRUCTIONS

1. Download the free App for iOS or Android
   (You can use the QR code or go to the store.)
2. Open the App on your Smartphone or Tablet
3. Point your camera at the rug on this page
4. Enjoy!

lunch at Haj Medi's farm, but excluded the episode of being tempted with the jewelry in the trunks and of seeing Parisian. I could smell commission, which was the driving force of the medina market, so I just kept what I had bought a secret.

I had become friends with a few of the waiters at the café. They were always aware of what people were wearing and willing to give them. Shoes, hats, jackets, belts—you name it, they needed it.

I paid for Ismael's breakfast and mine, said good-bye, and headed to my room to enjoy my new saddle rugs and then up to the terrace. I couldn't wait to clean them. Brecka was already heating up the water and starting to wash the sheets from the night before when I arrived. I told her I would like to clean my rugs and have her keep an eye on them while they dry.

When Brecka watched me unfold the saddle rugs, her eyes brightened, and she quickly left the terrace. A few minutes later she returned with a small black plastic bag that had a dark, gooey gob of something inside it. "What is this, Brecka?" I asked with a hint of alarm in my voice. "This is called *savon beldi*. It is made from olive oil, and it will clean and moisturize the wool without drying it out like Tide."

"OK," I said, and we submerged the pieces in the cauldron of now warm water. None of the colors ran, and we lightly scrubbed them so as not to damage the sequins, then hung them on the clothesline, where they would dry in the sun. Washing each, piece by piece, took the better part of the day. When Brecka left at three o'clock, the carpets were dry, and I gathered them up and took them back to my room.

I began packing them in my new army bag and realized that with the other small items I had bought, not everything was going to fit into my luggage. I sifted through my items, deciding what was essential for me to take back, what things I would give to the waiters, and planned to visit the "Jazz Man" store I had seen the other evening. While returning from the rug market, walking through a different alley, I had seen a lighted sign, "Jazz Man," that intrigued me. The store was closed, but looking through the window I saw an assortment of tourist leftovers, presumably from people who wanted to stay longer and needed some cash. I saw Western clothes, cameras, watches, tennis shoes, and Western music, all for sale.

I ended up taking a nap, and even though I seldom dreamed in the afternoon, this afternoon was different. All my experiences of the last few days were all jumbled together into one colorful dream. All the people's faces, the alleys, and the beggars pulling on me with their raggedy clothes and distorted bodies.

I woke to the call to prayer and set out to meet Jazz Man.

Apparently Jazz Man was only open in the evenings. I assumed that was when his customers came out too. He was just turning the key to his door when I approached. He looked like Picasso and wore a small goatee and long, stringy hair, black-and-white striped T-shirt, and white jeans. Delighted to see me, he immediately started grabbing and examining the clothes in my bag. He loved the tennis shoes, even though they stank, and treated like treasures a few of my surfing T-shirts with English wording. I also showed him two new baseball hats I had brought but never worn since they didn't help me fit in with Moroccans. He offered me a few dirhams and a little hash for my stuff. I told him I was leaving soon, so I wouldn't need the smoke, but I accepted the dirhams. I said, "I know I'll be coming back to Marrakech, and when I do, is there anything you would like me to bring?"

"Yes, Lawrence," he replied, "any American T-shirts in any size and color, but they must say 'Made in America.'"

"OK, Jazz Man, I will see you again."

Before I left my room to see the Jazz Man, I had decided to go back to the Iceberg for some Stork beer and my last shrimp omelet, and also to give Aziz one of my T-shirts. I knew enough about Moroccans by now to realize it was best to have the gift be more of a secret and not a big deal, so I rolled the shirt up in some paper and put it under my arm. Aziz was happy to see me, brought me the beer and omelet, and another free flan desert when I was finished. I told him that I was leaving the next day to return to America, but that I would be back as soon as possible and would not forget him. I gave him the paper package, we shook hands, and he kissed me on both cheeks. I then left the Iceberg to have one more experience of the

Djemma el Fna square at night.

I entered the square as things were already starting to happen. The perpetual commotion of snake charmers, acrobats, storytellers, and food vendors all created their own chaos, which I had come to love. I searched for my black plastic tarp and found it had moved a bit to the southern part of the square.

I observed a blind man being escorted by what looked like a young relative, perhaps his grandson, and he was attempting to sell his antique silver dagger. I had always loved these knives with all their history and thought this would make a wonderful last purchase. I approached the man and his grandson and started to bargain. I offered a fair price, and five minutes later I was in possession of the dagger. As I began happily walking back to the CTM Hotel, halfway there I got this tremendous feeling of guilt from buying the dagger from this blind man. I felt that a man's dagger, in this part of the world, would be the last thing of value he would sell. So I decided to return it to the owner. I quickly searched for them and found them eating in one of the portable restaurants. I returned the beautiful dagger to him, and with many hand gestures and broken English I finally got across that I didn't want my money back, that I wanted the blind gentleman to keep his dagger and my money too. I walked away feeling proud, thinking this was a good way to return all the generosity shown to me on this trip. I stood off to the side, looking back at the blind man and his grandson, to mark this memory. My good feelings didn't last long, however, because once they had finished eating their dinners, the blind man and his grandson approached another buyer who, after similar bargaining, purchased the dagger. I walked away disillusioned and feeling a bit naïve, and headed back to my hotel.

Wild, stray cats fighting in the alley had kept me awake most of the night. After waking early, I dressed and decided to avoid the Café de France my last day. I didn't want to see Ismael, explain what I had been up to, and have him hit me up for my last dirhams that I had gotten from Jazz Man. I went to Café du Progrès, which was next to Snake Hippies on Riad Zitone. A strange crew was already at the café. Many of the customers looked like they had spent the night there, drinking coffee and playing cards. I didn't make eye contact with any customers, had a quick kawa halib and croissant, and sneaked back into the hotel without anyone seeing me.

I went up to the terrace to help Brecka and to say my good-byes. "Brecka, is there anything you would like me to bring you from America?" She looked at me in her multilayered gauzy clothes, her soft eyes moist, and said, "Lawrence, I have never received a letter." I could never have imagined that this would be her answer, remembering my own mailbox at home, with all the advertisements and junk. I got out a piece of paper, and wrote down her address, vowing to myself that I would write her as soon as I got home. Brecka had helped me in so many ways, from the magical protective herbs to cleaning my stinky shoes, and I had never met anyone quite like her before, so old and wrinkled yet with such generosity. I kissed her on both cheeks and hurried downstairs.

Omar and La Hassan knew I would be leaving that day, but they let me have the room for a few free hours after the noon checkout time. I suspected both would be sad to see me go, and I was hoping to see them again too. Back in my room I took one last peek down at the alley, dressed in my American outfit I had been saving for the trip home, and carefully wrapped my yellow slippers in plastic and put them in the army duffle bag.

Moktar was waiting for me in the lobby, so I said quick good-byes to Omar and La Hassan, with handshakes and kisses on both cheeks. I told them I would return soon, and all three of us said "Enshalah" at the same time. La Hassan carried my bags to Moktar's car, and I slipped him a few dirhams in another handshake. With one last look at the square, I got in the passenger seat.

Moktar was a good driver and had the radio on. We didn't speak much on the drive; I think he knew I was wishing I could stay longer in his country and wanted to be left to my own thoughts. As we entered Casablanca, the traffic intensified, but Moktar knew exactly where to go. He joined the cars and motorbikes heading toward the train station, and a few blocks beyond the station we parked directly across the street from a flower market, and I saw the sign for the Colbert Hotel.

We entered the lobby, and I realized this was not a hotel for tourists, especially not foreign Christians. Everyone I saw, and they were all men, wore full-length white garments, looking like they were on their way to Mecca. They gave me barely disguised dirty looks as Moktar and I approached the desk. The desk man refused to look at me, and only after a rather heated exchange in Arabic between Moktar and him, in which I heard the name Ahmed Karbush several times, did he grudgingly give me a key. Moktar told me he would be back to pick me up at eight a.m. to take me to the airport. I think he was happy to leave the Colbert Hotel.

I walked up the narrow stairway, opened the door to my room, and looked around. I had certainly been given the worst room they had, Ahmed Karbush or not. The bed was so soft and had such a large dip in the center that it could have been a hammock. The bathroom had a filthy shower and a so-called modern toilet, but without any kind of seat, and the only thing besides the bed was a broken chair. I knew this was going to be a very long night, but I took out a book and some smoked almonds and read until I finally fell asleep on the horrible bed. I never took off my clothes or got under the bedspread or sheets, certain there might be bed bugs waiting to eat me.

I woke in the early morning, opened the wooden shutters, and could smell the flowers from the market. Then I saw Moktar's old diesel Mercedes parked under my second story window. Now knowing that Moktar was close by, I cleaned up quickly, grabbed my duffel bag and the rest of my belongings, left the key in the door, and walked downstairs. There were already a few men sitting in the lobby, looking like they had been there all night; maybe the management just rented them chairs. No one said good morning, and I exited the nondescript front door. Looking both ways, I saw a nearby café, knowing that Moktar must be close by. When I entered, sitting in the corner against a mosaic tile wall was Moktar. He ordered two sandwiches to go: mashed potatoes, hard-boiled eggs, vinegar, onions, and olive oil, all in a French baguette wrapped in newsprint. We ate the sandwiches as we drove out of town to the airport. On the way I noticed a lot of security and military personnel everywhere, and remembered that they had holsters but no guns. Moktar dropped me off, wished me a safe flight, and I stepped inside to begin the journey home.

❧ Chapter Four ❧

NYC to SPI

⬦⬦⬦⬦⬦⬦⬦⬦⬦⬦⬦⬦⬦⬦⬦⬦⬦⬦⬦⬦⬦⬦⬦⬦

THE FLIGHT TO NEW YORK WAS ON TIME and not crowded, so I got a seat in the back of the plane, stretched out, and was able to sleep most of the way. As we approached New York, everyone but the Americans were glued to the windows. I knew they had never seen a city as big as this, and they all must be a little nervous.

Since I was at the rear of the plane, I had to pass all the rows to exit. Each row looked like a garbage dump. The Moroccans had just thrown on the floor anything and everything. The supplied blankets and pillows, socks and eye covers, were all strewn on the floor. Many passengers had apparently brought some of their favorite foods from home, judging from the empty plastic bags that had been filled with items like cookies and dates and were lying near mounds of plastic water bottles. I felt sorry for the cleanup crew who worked for Royal Air Maroc.

I joined the other passengers, all walking toward immigration. There was a long escalator that took you from the second floor down to where you collected your baggage and then went through customs. One older woman, dressed in her finest djellaba, got close to the movable escalator steps, and then got out of line, visibly scared. She did this again and again, moving up to the stairs and then turning away. Another Moroccan woman, perhaps well-traveled, finally took her hand and led her onto the escalator. The whole ordeal created quite a traffic jam since there was only one escalator for all the passengers.

Once I finally made it down to the baggage carousels, I saw my military duffle bag and my other bag revolving around. As I was waiting for my bags to reach me, a custom agent who was leading a beagle—presumably used for drug sniffing—came up to me and asked me to go to line 2. I nodded and then glanced over at line 2 to see a young African American woman painstakingly looking through everyone's luggage. I waited until the agent wandered off, grabbed my bags, and looked for another agent. Four lanes down was an older man, looking like he might be getting ready to retire. He was just waving the passengers through, so I selected him. When it was my turn, he motioned for me to put my bags on the table, asked me where I was coming from, what I had spent, and what I had bought.

I told him Marrakech, Morocco, two hundred dollars, and some old blankets. Before he said anything else, I asked him how the Yankees were doing. I must have hit on his favorite subject. He forgot about looking in my bags and told me the Yankees were a bunch of bums, welcomed me back to America, and waved me on.

Once I was outside customs, there were many chauffeurs holding up paper signs with people's names printed on them. I navigated through that group and found an exit with a bus stop sign that read "Shuttle to rental cars." I waited just a short while and boarded the next bus. Getting off at the Hertz rental car lot outside the airport, I walked a short way back to the entrance and stuck out my thumb. It didn't take long before a man picked me up who was traveling between airports on his way to Newark. I told him a little about my travels, and he let me off at the highway outside the exit to the Newark airport.

By then the sun was going down, and I hoped I could catch a ride before it got any later. As I looked around, this appeared to be a bad part of town. After I had waited an hour, a car slowed down, passed me, and then started to back up. As it neared me, I saw that the passengers seemed dangerous, like they might be thugs. They stopped near me and began filing out of the car. At that moment another car stopped and the driver yelled at me to hurry up and get in—perfect timing. I ran to his car and jumped in. Before he asked me where I was going, he asked if I was in the military. I guess he had seen my army duffle bag and presumed I must be in the service. I told him I had just come from Morocco and was on my way back to my college. He said he was on a short leave from the Coast Guard and lived about an hour south of Newark. He then asked if I needed a place to stay for the night, offering his home.

I answered, "Sure, why not?" thinking that whatever might happen, it was better than being back with the dangerous thugs he had rescued me from.

He said his name was Pete, and we chatted back and forth until we arrived at his two-story home. It was modestly furnished, clean, and comfortable. We drank a few beers together, and before he went to his bedroom he told me he had an early morning appointment and would take me back to the interstate on his way.

Exhausted from the trip, I lay down on his couch. Suddenly I sat up, startled by the realization that until this point I had completely forgotten about the $8,000 hidden in my money belt. I understood then how easily I could have been robbed, and I thanked God for the army bag that made Pete think I was in the service and prompted him to pick me up.

Pete woke me up as the sun was rising. We had a quick coffee together and then, as promised, he took me to the interstate. I thanked him for helping me, and after he drove off, I stuck my thumb out. It didn't take too long before a white Dodge panel van stopped, and a woman on the passenger side asked me where I was going. I just said, "South." "Come on in," so I opened the sliding door and entered. Once inside I realized it was like a cargo van with a metal screen that separated you from the front passengers. The driver was a heavy-set man who looked strong, about thirty years old, and the woman had really long hair and wore an even longer dress. She right away began to ask me about Jesus and being saved.

This went on for quite a while, and both would quote the Bible at different times. I kept telling them I just wanted to go back to college, get my car, and drive to South Texas. They, however, had other plans. The door had been locked from the outside when I closed it, and the metal screen kept me imprisoned in the back. They repeatedly said, "Come with us to our religious commune and find Jesus." I responded again and again that while I did believe in God, I just wanted to continue my education and make up my own mind. Somewhere in Virginia, they must have decided between the two of them to give up on me, so they stopped the van in the middle of nowhere. She opened the door from the outside and told me to get out, saying I wasn't worth being saved.

Surrounded by pine trees on Interstate 95, I finally got picked up by a man in his late thirties driving a brand-new Cadillac.

"Where are you headed?" he asked.

"Knoxville, Tennessee."

"I'm going to Ashville, North Carolina. Would you be willing to help me drive?"

I said yes, feeling very lucky, and got in the car. We got along fabulously. He had a keen interest in hearing about my trip to Morocco and asked what was in my duffle bag. I told him just some cheap gifts and dirty clothes. He was a rep for a carpet company from Hyde Point, North Carolina, and was driving back from doing a show in New York City. How strange this seemed, so I told him about all the carpets I had seen in Marrakech but never mentioned buying any.

Since I shared the driving, we drove all through the night, rarely stopping except for gas, and by the next evening he dropped me off in front of my friends' apartment, much to their surprise. Mark and Sandra had been raised in Saudi Arabia because both their families were working for Aramco Oil Company. Oddly enough, they had met, not in Saudi Arabia, but at college, and had been a couple ever since. They were so happy to see me that Mark immediately brought out the ouzo to celebrate my return.

After several salutes with ouzo, they asked about my trip. They had known I was going to Morocco, and we had spent many a night talking about my plans for my surfing adventure before I left. The three of us had been art majors together, so I knew that what was in my duffle bag would be much appreciated.

While I began showing the saddle rugs, there was a knock on the door. Sandra opened it, and standing there was my old college sweetheart, Donna Dougan. She had called them while I was gone, and they said I had called from Marrakech and told them when I might be back. By this time we had switched from the ouzo to beer, and the storytelling continued late into the night.

Mark and Sandra finally said good-night and left us alone. Donna then told me she had missed me. She stripped down to nothing and just stood naked in the living room. Her best features were her beautiful large breasts and long brown hair that now fell across her shoulders. I took her hand and led her down the hall to the extra bedroom. Small as it was, they had managed to fit in a queen-size bed. Donna kissed me a few times, placed her head on my shoulder, and told me again how much she had missed me since we had broken up. Donna had never been very good at sex, and I believed she really didn't like it. We made love and then fell asleep exhausted and sweaty, having made plans to get together again the next evening.

We both awoke with small hangovers from the ouzo and found Mark and Sandra already up and drinking strong, black Arabian coffee that they had brought with them from Saudi. Donna had a job as a teacher of children with learning disabilities and needed to leave soon, and I needed to get my car, which had been parked in underground parking at a friend's apartment complex while I was gone. After a few more gulps of coffee, we said good-bye to Mark and Sandra and exited hand in hand, looking forward to another night of old friendship.

At the apartment complex I jumped into my VW bug convertible and drove to an auto parts store to pick up oil and all else required to get the car back in service. I spent the rest of the day changing oil and cleaning up my car, and then just lay around waiting for Mark and Sandra to get home. When they arrived, I told them Donna was coming over again, so we decided on a restaurant that had been an old hangout for the four of us.

We had already started on an early happy hour when Donna again appeared at the front door. Dressed to kill, she seemed to be trying to make a great last impression. We had broken up months before when she realized I wanted a life filled with adventure, and she wanted a home and family in Jackson, Tennessee. We had a great time at the restaurant. All of us had been friends for a few years and enjoyed each other's company immensely.

The sex that night was a little better, as she tried out a few more of her moves. We held each other for a long time, knowing this might be our last night together. In the morning I gathered up my small carpets that had been spread around the apartment and put them in the army duffle bag. As we were all drinking more of the strong Arabian coffee, I glanced over at Donna and noticed small tears forming in her eyes. We had been classmates, best friends, lovers, and roommates, and this morning was sad for both of us. I knew I had a better chance of seeing Mark and Sandra in Saudi Arabia than Donna in Jackson, Tennessee. Mark and Sandra planned to return to Saudi after graduate school, get married, and work for Aramco like their parents. Donna had to go to work then, Mark and Sandra had classes, so we all stood and hugged one another. I left first, smiled, and never looked back.

I had always believed change was necessary, and I wasn't afraid of it. I drove down Cumberland Boulevard past the liquor store I had managed for a few years, and a few tears dropped down my face. I looked in the rearview mirror and saw the silhouette of the Smokey Mountains. It was then I knew that I was leaving the past behind, that I was on my way to a whole new experience, and most important, that I was ready for it.

Heading due west on Interstate 40, I stopped to put the top down on the convertible and locked the carpets in the trunk. With the wind blowing through my hair, I felt no pain, just freedom.

I had my college diploma, a few clothes, and two wooden sculptures I had created in my art classes. Those two I cherished and had not been able to give away with the rest of my pieces. Along with my duffle bag full of rugs, everything I ever owned or wanted fit in the back seat and trunk of my car.

As I approached Nashville, I turned the rock 'n' roll station off and found a good country-western station that I listened to until I crossed the state line and entered Mississippi. Huge cotton plantations were on both sides of the highway, as well as small wooden shacks grouped together with paint peeling off and porches with swings, but no one around.

I drove on another hour and stopped at a honky-tonk with a large Confederate flag painted on the billboard advertising chicken fried steak and hush puppies. I was hungry by then, and I'd always loved chicken fried steak. A few motorcycles and an old GMC pickup were parked out front. I parked by the front screen door so I could keep my eye on my VW since the top was still down.

A waitress, who looked like she had eaten too much peach pie, came over and asked me what I wanted to eat and where I was headed. I said, "Chicken fried steak and hush puppies," and told her I was on my way to South Texas near the Mexican border. She began to tell me that she trusted the Mexicans less than the blacks, and that she thought they were all thieves and dangerous.

A few redneck types wandered in and asked me what I was doing here. One wanted to know if I was with the NAACP. I told them I was just a college student from Tennessee, going south to Texas to work in the oil fields. With that answer, they simply turned around and forgot about me. *Well, that was a lucky answer to give*, I thought as I felt the money belt around my waist, and then ate quickly and got the hell out of there.

Back on the road and continuing south, I crossed the Mississippi River and saw barges being towed up and down the waterway, heading from New Orleans all the way up to Minneapolis and back. Most of them were flat barges being pushed by massive tug boats. The fish flies spattered my windshield as I crossed the bridge, and I wished I had put my top up on my VW bug.

Later in the afternoon, I began looking for an icehouse to buy a few cold beers. Up ahead was a billboard advertising one that promised the coldest beers in Louisiana, so I couldn't wait to get there.

I sat on a bench outside on the covered patio with several ceiling fans revolving overhead and drank two beers, ice cold as promised, but wrapped in toilet paper. I presumed they thought it would keep the beer colder, but I just peeled it off. I bought another for the road and then searched for a state park or rest area to spend the night.

An hour later as it was beginning to get dark, I saw a sign that said "Rest Area." I picked a spot somewhat hidden by some trees, brushed my teeth, put the top up on my car, and pulled my sleeping bag out of the trunk. I drank my beer, and then fell asleep on one of the wooden picnic tables. Waking up while it was still dark, I knew I would be in Houston before nightfall.

I arrived in Lafayette, Louisiana, around lunchtime, so I had a muffuletta sandwich at a truck stop on Interstate 10. I decided to call my parents and Ahmed Karbush's son and tell them I'm on my way. I reached my mother and got directions since I had never visited them in this home in Houston before, but could only leave a message at the dorm for Ismael Karbush.

From Lafayette to Lake Charles a seemingly endless system of small bridges passed over a series of swamps and lagoons. Once I crossed into Texas, there was a steady stream of tractor trailer trucks all carrying oil-field equipment. The outskirts of Houston must have extended more than fifty miles since I was last there. The downtown intersections were confusing, but I was still able to navigate it with the instructions my mother had given me.

Once I arrived at my parents' home, they were eager to hear about my travels to Morocco. Extremely well-traveled, they seemed to have been to just about everywhere in the world at least once. I guess I had it in my blood too. I never mentioned buying the carpets or the courier service I was performing for Ahmed Karbush, because I knew they would just be negative. They were still angry at me for deciding not to go to graduate school. Surfing and Morocco, to them, was just a waste of time—an interlude before I had to get serious about life and start a career. I told them I was looking forward to getting to South Padre Island and start working with my friend Gary, who I had known for years.

I stayed with my parents only one night. In the morning I was able to reach Ismael Karbush at the dorm before he left for class. We arranged to meet at the student center around noon. The University of Houston is in the downtown area of the city, so it wasn't difficult to find. I pulled into the visitor parking and went looking for the student center and someone who looked Moroccan. As I approached the student center, I saw Ismael, who looked remarkably like his father, sitting near the entrance. After we greeted each other, I pulled the money envelope from my front pocket and handed it to Ismael. He asked me to join him for a coffee and inquired about his family and Marrakech.

After about an hour I politely told him I needed to get on my way to South Padre. I requested that he count the money and then make a telephone call right then to tell his father I had delivered it. I didn't want any problems, ever, between Ahmed Karbush and me. Also, frankly, I felt there were several times since New York where I might have been robbed and was lucky I hadn't. Now I simply wanted the whole thing completed. Ismael did as I asked and counted the money, then we went to find a telephone where I heard him speak to his father. We shook hands, I wished him luck with his studies—"Enshalah"—and off I went to get back on the road with my VW bug.

I looked at my map and thought the drive from Houston to South Padre Island would be about six hours. I called Gary and left a message, telling him of my pending arrival. Having gotten seriously lost while leaving the city, I only made it to Corpus Christi before it got too dark. I found a restaurant with some giant Gulf Coast shrimp, and then slept on the beach in my sleeping bag. I got up with the sunrise and continued south.

South Padre is a three-hour trip from Corpus, and for one and a half of those three I drove through the massive King Ranch, which has over 825,000 acres and was founded in 1853. Approaching the island, I went over a mile-long extension bridge from the mainland. The island itself resembled a narrow sand bar. Driving around on the island, I noticed a lot of beach homes built on telephone pole stilts, and also what appeared to be a newly built Hyatt Regency Hotel, as well as some seafood restaurants on the Back Bay.

On the main drag, the only paved road, I noticed a restaurant with the sign "The Donut Hole." I parked my VW, thinking that if anyone knew where I could find Gary, it would be someone working there since Gary always liked to eat breakfast out. By then the breakfast crowd had already left, and there were only a few hangers-on drinking iced tea—the drink of choice since it was already so hot in the late morning. I looked around and saw a young, tanned, pretty waitress who I figured would know Gary. I guessed right. She said he lived down the beach in one of the largest homes, adding that I couldn't miss it because it also had a gigantic telescope on the roof, used for star-gazing parties. I easily found the home with her directions, and then went looking for his job site.

Not far from the restaurant, perched on a sand dune near the water, an extended cab Chevrolet truck had a sign on the driver's side that read Island Contractors, license #22784. On the roof of a two-story beach house was Gary, working only in cutoff jeans and tennis shoes.

He immediately recognized my red VW convertible because we had numerous double dates in my car. He was genuinely happy to see me; I could see the grin on his face. He climbed down the ladder and gave me a solid handshake and multiple hugs and pats on the back.

Gary had hired four Mexican men—all brothers from Matamoras. Each man came over to introduce themselves. The oldest was named Six-Toe, a big guy with a large droopy mustache who looked like he knew what he was doing, and the other brothers probably took his lead. Gary told me to meet him at his beach house after work at four o'clock. He said we had lots to catch up on and wanted to hear all my stories of Morocco and what had happened with Donna.

I drove down to the opposite end of the island to the Jetties. I discovered a large restaurant with plate glass windows facing the ocean, and around back a small, dark, seedy bar. I picked the bar to spend a few hours before Gary got off work. The bar backed up on the intercoastal, a canal that went to the port of Brownsville. Across the inlet lay Mexico, so close you could swim or paddle a surfboard there. I ordered iced tea and a plate of fried and cold boiled shrimp.

Relaxing by the window with the air conditioners rattling, I realized this island was an extremely hot place in the summer. It was the end of June, and I still had to be prepared for the increased heat of July, August, and September. I suspected they started work at around six in the morning, took off for a siesta in the heat of the day, and then worked until four. A few driftwood characters wandered in and out for a couple of cold beers, and some appeared intent on finding someone, maybe looking to score. It seemed like this was a place that had witnessed numerous drug deals go down.

I dozed off and was awakened by the bartender, who told me his shift was over and he needed to clean out his register. I looked at my watch; it was almost time to meet Gary at his house. I had neglected to put up the convertible top to my car, and the black upholstery seats were red hot.

Driving back north on the beach road, I could see the tall telescope from a distance. Gary was already there, taking some building materials from the back of his truck. I pulled up and without saying anything gave him a hand. We had worked together for two summers building apartments in Knoxville, so we instantly anticipated each other's moves and worked well together. Gary was a few inches taller and heavier, and as tan as a coffee bean.

We walked up the stairs, and he immediately turned on the air conditioning. It was obvious that without the cool air, one couldn't live here. Gary's beautifully furnished home had a large kitchen, a living room with leather sectionals, two full baths, and a panoramic view of the ocean. Gary's bedroom was the larger of the two rooms, and the second one appeared to be occupied. I guessed that Gary had a roommate, which he did, but he explained that by next week his friend would be moving from the beach back to Brownsville where he had his main home.

He opened the icebox, which was full of Mexican beers, and invited me to sit down and tell him all about my new adventures. Gary was an interested listener, so I talked for at least an hour about Morocco, hitchhiking from New York, carrying the $8,000 to Houston in my money belt and the ten small saddle rugs locked in my trunk. We had often talked about traveling around the world, but so far only I had seized the opportunity.

The full moon was rising over the ocean, making the beach sand seem even whiter. It was time for dinner and drinks at his favorite Back Bay restaurant, Louie's Backyard. Gary mentioned that he had become friends with Louie, the owner, by building his boat dock and private club last year, so we should be able to get a table and a few free drinks. We walked over since it was just a few blocks away.

Louie saw us immediately as we walked to the outside palapa bar. The specialties were margaritas and piña coladas served in an oversized punch glass. Gary introduced me to Louie, an older man, well dressed in a blue blazer with brass buttons, white slacks, and a T-shirt that had a boat dock stenciled on it with the name Louie's.

Unmistakably gay, he shook my hand a little too long.

When a table vacated, we had already finished two of the margaritas and were discussing Gary's construction business. He was doing well on the island. He had his contractor's license and kept all his tools and equipment in a store locker across the bridge. Turning down business because he had no one else to take on the extra responsibilities, he was interested to know when I wanted to start. Gary said he could put together another team of workers for me who were all related to Six-Toe. These young and talented Mexicans would always show up and work hard, but never on weekends even if it was for more money.

Louie's restaurant was buffet-style, so the waiters only served the cocktails and, rarely, coffee. We stood in line behind two good-looking blonds with deep suntans. As I reached to fill my plate with fried shrimp and some seafood au gratin, our eyes met and she smiled at me, so I asked her where she was from. "The Big D," she replied, "Dallas, Texas, near Turtle Creek." Standing there with her hands full, she asked me where I was from, and I told her I had just returned from Marrakech, Morocco, where I had intended to go surfing, but since there wasn't any surf in the summer, I had spent my time wandering the medina shopping for antiques instead. I suspected she wanted to hear more, so I invited both women to join Gary and me.

The food at Louie's was delicious. Fresh gulf shrimp and grouper fingers were the specialty, and the Caesar salad was tasty. The girls introduced themselves as June and Taylor. Both were in medical school to become nurses and had less than a year left before graduation. For the last three years they came down to South Padre and rented a condo on the beach for summer break. They also said neither one of them had any time for boyfriends back home because of school.

My stories of Morocco intrigued Taylor more than June, and she adjusted her seat to sit closer to me. During our conversations Louie came up to Gary and invited all of us to a private party he was throwing at the new Hyatt Regency starting at eleven o'clock. Gary decided not to attend because he had to get up early to work the next day, but the girls were eager to go and so was I. Gary left about ten, telling me he would leave the front door open. June, Taylor, and I hung around the palapa bar and then walked over to the Hyatt. Louie's Backyard was the happening social place on the island, so his private party was well attended.

He had an open bar where at least half of his guests were mulling around or propping themselves up by holding onto the bar. The rest were lying around the pool, grabbing drinks from trays as the waiters strolled around. When we first arrived, Louie was nowhere to be found, but eventually he showed up with a few more guests. He walked around, thanking people for coming, and then headed over to our table by the pool.

Louie wasn't interested in June or Taylor; it was me he was directing his questions to. When he asked where I had come from, I told him also that I had been in Marrakech, had just graduated from college, and was down on the island to see my college buddy, Gary, and work on construction with him.

Louie asked me question after question about Morocco because he had always wanted to go there, loved the fashion of Yves Saint Laurent, who owned a villa in Marrakech and was influenced by Moroccan style, and hoped one day to open a Moroccan restaurant in Tampa, Florida, where he was from. He then asked me if I owned a blue blazer, which surprised me because it was the only sport jacket I did own. When I answered yes, he quickly offered me a job at his restaurant as the maître d'. He told me I would make a great deal more money working at Louie's for the rest of the season and could build beach houses after the tourist season was over. It was tempting, so I said I would think about it and come over to see him later in the week.

We were all full of margaritas and Mexican beer, and as we stood up to leave, both June and Taylor grabbed each of my hands and led me out of the hotel. We walked over to Gary's where we jumped into my convertible and headed up the beach to their condo. I didn't know what to expect but figured it was going to be fun. It was.

I stayed with June and Taylor the entire week, eating at Louie's in the evening and the Donut Hole for breakfast. Both girls liked me, so I spent time jumping back and forth between bedrooms. When their beach vacation ended, we all hugged and kissed and made plans to maybe get together in the future and do it all over again. All this time I had been seeing Gary, not at Louie's, but at the Donut Hole. He would be leaving about the time the three of us wandered in. I hadn't made up my mind yet about working at Louie's, but I did think it would be fun since there were always lots of parties—and girls on vacation.

Gary's roommate, Hector, had moved back to Brownsville about the time the girls left for Dallas, so the timing was excellent and I moved into Gary's second bedroom. I started to work for Gary the next morning and teamed up with Six-Toe and his *primos*, cousins, to finish building the beach house while Gary started a new project.

Gary had perfected a method of building these beach homes called box building. Once we got the telephone poles in the ground, we leveled them, bolting down the floor joists and nailing down the deck. Building the walls, putting in the windows and doors, all of that was done with the materials lying on the deck so we didn't need any ladders or scaffolding. For the first two or three weeks it looked like we were doing nothing, then we would get everyone to help us and suddenly the walls were raised. All we had to do then was build the stairs, and the house was ready for the electricians and plumbers.

Getting up at six a.m. did not help my social life. I had been back to Louie's a few times—the most happening place on the island after the sun went down. It was always crowded, and there wasn't much on the island to compete with it. The more I hung out at Louie's, the more I was interested in taking his offer to work there. Always polite, Louie was a fantastic front man, introducing himself to every customer.

One night I went back and was told Louie was on the boat dock. Seeing me, he called me over and asked, "Come to apply for the job?"

"How did you know?"

"Just guessing," he said with a smile. "You must guarantee me that you will stay to work through Labor Day, starting tomorrow with no days off, seven days a week."

I agreed and left thinking how lucky I was. I had not been on the island for very long, and now I had two jobs. All I needed were the white pants and white tennis shoes, so the next morning I drove to

Brownsville to buy them. Louie supplied the T-shirts and hats.

Working both jobs would soon become difficult. I started work at Louie's at four p.m. and worked till eleven, and then usually went to Champions across the bridge to drink and dance. After a few weeks I was ready for a major change at Louie's. I had gotten the maître d' job down pat and decided I wanted more work and more money. So one hot afternoon before the guests arrived, I asked Louie to give me the six tables at the dock overlooking the Back Bay. Two other waiters had been serving there but had been caught stealing money from the restaurant. Their method had worked for most of the summer until Louie saw them shuffling around two different receipt books. One was used for credit cards and the other for cash. Louie observed them putting the cash in their pockets, so now the six tables were open. Louie said, "Go for it, but do not steal from me."

I had never worked as a waiter before, so I looked around and chose a young boy to be my helper and instructor. His name was Danny, and he had been busing tables there for over a year and knew everyone. Choosing Danny was a great stroke of luck for me, and he helped me learn the ropes. Louie's also had a steel drum band that would never quit, and everyone would do the limbo. I made a deal with Danny that if he would practice the limbo after school, I would start betting on him and we would split it, and both of us would make more money. We never lost, but it always looked like we might to that cheerleader daughter from Dallas. The limbo band was wild, and people at the restaurant were eager to try to bend lower and lower under the limbo pole. Soon the whole restaurant staff was in the limbo line, and Danny was beating everyone while making it look like he was just lucky. One night we made $120 each just by betting on limbo.

One of the secrets to Louie's success was the amount of alcohol he put in the drinks. Many people would get totally wasted and begin betting on the limbo contests. Louie loved it, and he just kept serving the liquor. He knew the limbo and gambling kept the customers drinking more and eating less.

One day he asked me why I didn't serve any coffee or desserts. He knew I was sending my customers to the Dairy Queen up the street. I said, "Look how many times I turn these tables."

There were lots of tips to be made because you didn't have to share your earnings, although it did end up helping me to give a portion of my tips to the bartender. The bartender was Lindsey from Austin, Texas, and she was also the assistant manager. I soon became friends with her by helping her at the bar and at closing. After I knew her a bit more, I invited her over and showed her the Moroccan saddle rugs I had hidden in my closet. Lindsey had an art degree from the University of Texas in Austin and showed a great deal of appreciation and love for the weavings. Lindsey told me she had a boyfriend, Pierre, who owned an art gallery in New Orleans, saying he was coming to town tomorrow and would probably be interested in seeing my rugs. Lindsey said I should come with my duffle bag a few hours before Louie's opened, and she would introduce us.

As I waited at Louie's with my saddle rugs, I sat out by the pier to think about what I should try to sell them for. I started to think about my stay in Marrakech and what an impression it had made on me. The hot sun, even though I was under an umbrella, must have cooked my brain, because I decided to offer the rugs for ten times what I had paid for them and see if he was interested.

Lindsey showed up without her boyfriend but offered to drive me to his house. She drove one of the old VW Things, army green and totally rusted out. She told me it never left the island; I doubted that it could have. As we pulled up to his beach house below the sand dunes, I saw a new, black Dodge Ram van with tinted windows and oversized tires. I looked up to see a man dressed in a judo outfit staring out the window at us. Pierre came to the door and invited us in.

I set the duffle bag on the floor by the entry. The beach house was beautiful, decorated with antique Mexican masks on the walls and Oaxacan rugs on the floors. He asked me a few questions, such as where I had bought them, and if I owned them. I thought this was an interesting question. Pierre then began taking them out of the duffle bag as gently as I had put them in. As he looked at each one, his eyes began to sparkle like he knew what he was searching for. He inspected each of the ten pieces, and then wasting no time, Pierre asked me how much I wanted for all ten. This caught me by surprise, but it was just what I had wanted to happen. "Ten thousand," I said. Pierre stood up and told me to follow him. We walked over to the refrigerator, and he opened the freezer and pulled out a stack of money wrapped in cellophane. He counted out $10,000 all in hundreds, and then asked me to count it again, just like in Morocco.

I asked Pierre if I could keep the duffle bag, remembering that it had saved me on the hitchhiking experience from JFK, and he said he wouldn't need it. Walking back down the stairs, I was already missing my weavings, but the cold money in my pocket made me happier.

Later at Louie's that night Lindsay didn't ask for anything and said she was happy Pierre and I had met. I asked around and found out that Pierre was also in the marijuana-trafficking business. He traveled to the island once a month, loaded up his Dodge Ram van, and drove at night when the customs check was closed at the King Ranch. I really couldn't have cared less how he made his money, but I knew I would never forget the cold one-hundred-dollar bills from the icebox.

After selling the saddle rugs to Pierre and waiting tables at Louie's, I really didn't need to work construction for Gary. I stayed on for two more weeks so I could help him finish one of his many homes on the sand dunes. Gary totally understood, and we remained friends and roommates.

I now had a few dollars—the money from the rugs and the additional money I was making at Louie's—so I opened a checking account and rented a safety deposit box at a small branch bank called Beach Savings and Loan on the other side of the causeway at Port Isabel. I started to party less and save more. I now realized what I could do with this money in Morocco. I started thinking maybe I was just lucky, but then again I knew Pierre would have never bought them without knowing he could sell them in his art gallery for much more money than what he had paid for them. I began to plan my next trip back to Morocco, remembering I had an agreement with Louie to stay the season.

All days became the same, a little busier on the weekends, and there hadn't been any surf to speak of—miserable, in fact, no waves, just a flat ocean surface—and the sand was way too hot to walk or run on.

I was taking a nap before starting work at four, when I woke to the telephone ringing. I answered, and a girl's voice asked for Hector. I said he didn't live here anymore, and she sounded disappointed, so I asked her if I could help. She said her name was Heidi, that her mother was a friend of Hector's, and that she and her friend were on the island for the weekend. Her mother had told her that Hector would tell them the fun places to go. I introduced myself and invited her to come to Louie's for dinner, saying I worked there.

During the evening rush Heidi and her friend came in. Heidi was a tall blond with blue eyes who commanded attention. Her friend Linda was closer to my size, with reddish-blond hair and dark brown eyes. I ushered them to a great table on the water and talked to them a little bit when I wasn't too busy. They both were laughing and having fun. I mentioned that my roommate and I were hosting one of our full-moon star-gazing parties and invited them to come by our beach house after I got off work.

Our star-gazing parties had become a rather epic event every month, and this one was no exception. Most of the other staff from Louie's were there, along with tourists we'd invited and some of Gary's contractor friends. When Gary had rented the beach house, the huge telescope on the roof came with it, so he had started these full-moon parties months before. The parties started late, normally after ten, and often lasted until the early hours of the morning when it finally cooled off. I noticed Heidi and Linda climbing the stairs to the patio where the party was now in full swing, and everyone was waiting to look through the telescope at the full moon. Two pretty girls were always welcome at a party, and I introduced them around. They were talkative and friendly, and everyone was having a good time.

After an hour or so I saw Linda sitting alone on the large swing on the deck and sat down with her. While swinging back and forth I realized she was interesting and found myself telling her about Morocco, some of my dreams after Louie's job ended, and a bit about myself. Linda then told her story of recently moving to Brownsville from Denver, how she didn't know anyone and had moved here to help her mother who had just had back surgery. She mentioned that

Heidi was married to her older brother and was only there for the weekend, whereas she didn't know how long she would be in Brownsville.

We talked for quite a while, and people started leaving the party. I excused myself to thank everyone for coming. Heidi and Linda joined those leaving. I told them I had enjoyed meeting them, gave them names of some other restaurants and places to go, and told Linda to stop by again when she was back on the island. I hadn't realized what a crowd of people were there until I saw how many were exiting onto the sandy streets. A few of my waiter friends had told me to look beyond the driftwood tourist girls for some local ones for the winter. But I had no interest; I wasn't going to be on the island by then.

Chapter Five

Knock on the Door

◇◇

ABOUT THREE WEEKS LATER, in the middle of the afternoon, I heard a knock on my door. Who would ever believe that a single knock on a screen door would change your life forever? I had been extremely lucky my whole life, and now I opened the door and standing there, unbeknown to me then, was the person who would one day be my wife. I opened it up and saw Linda, the girl from the swing, who had been on the island jogging the beach and had decided to stop by. I told her to give me a minute, changed clothes, grabbed the keys to my VW bug, and took her to the Jetties bar-restaurant. Settling into a booth, watching the dolphins, drinking a few cold beers, and eating fried gulf shrimp, we continued our conversation. Too soon I had to go back home to get ready for work, but this time I got her telephone number. She intrigued me, and I wanted to get to know her better.

A few days later I called, and Linda mentioned that she and her parents were planning to eat out for dinner at Port Isabel and invited me to join them after I finished at Louie's. Meeting the parents can make anyone nervous, but Linda's were unique. Her mother, Betty, was gentle and beautiful, with the same reddish hair and dark brown eyes as Linda's, and her father, Paul, was a successful trial attorney, very Irish, one who lived life to the fullest, laughed often, and was quite generous. We were all having a great time, laughing and talking, when Paul asked me about my college life and what I had studied. I told him art and mentioned that I had some of my sculptures with me at my beach house. He then got the check and said, "Let's go see them."

Out in the parking lot, when he spied my VW bug convertible, he declared that he wanted to ride with me and have "the girls" follow in his Mercedes. Paul climbed into the passenger seat, and once we started over the bridge he turned to me and said, "Let's go as fast as we can, and if we get caught, I will split the ticket with you." I had never met anyone quite like him, and I realized right then that not only did his daughter intrigue me, so, too, did her father.

Linda and I continued going out. Sometimes I would drive to Brownsville, other times she would drive to the island. Her father had an International 4 x 4, which he drove to a camp to hunt white wing and snow geese in the marshes south of Matamoras. This hunting truck, which she would drive to meet me on the island, had huge steer horns mounted to the front, and the car horn played Banda, Mexican ranchero music. The first time I was invited to her parents' home for dinner, I got lost trying to find the house on the golf course at the country club, and Linda had to walk to the clubhouse parking lot to find me. That night Paul served me my very first filet mignon steak, and when he saw how much I liked it, it was always on the menu whenever I came for dinner.

Labor Day was approaching, and the tourist season on the island was winding down. I had told Louie I would work every day until Labor Day, and I had kept my word. With the money I saved from working at Louie's, combined with the money from selling my saddle rugs to the drug dealer, I knew I had more than enough to return to Marrakech. What I also knew was that I wanted Linda to come with me.

Although she was not well-traveled, Linda had gone to Acapulco a few times, so I knew she had a passport. I had already learned she was a good sport about things, so more than likely an easy traveler. Morocco would require being both. I decided that on our next date I would ask her to come with me. Her parents would have some reservations about her going, but since I had been there before, I could talk them into letting their daughter go. I succeeded. Linda would become an excellent companion and traveler. She never complained and traveled light.

Royal Air Maroc had discontinued the direct flight from JFK to Marrakech, and now they only flew to Casablanca. Back then, before more Moroccans started coming to the States, the flights were always half empty; you could easily find four empty seats in the middle rows at the back of the plane once it took off. It was always an easy flight leaving New York around 7:00 p.m. and arriving as the sun was rising. They always served the same food, Moroccan-style chicken or beef, which I never liked, so I would give my plate to some hungry Moroccan and only eat the bread with butter, and the cream cheese on crackers. In the early days they had an open bar, where all the Moroccans would crowd around for the whole flight. The smoking section of the plane was filled with heavy cigarette smoke, and the nonsmoking section directly in front of it wasn't much better. Years later I learned how to disconnect the smoke alarm in the bathroom and would smoke a joint before the meal was served.

Linda and I were on the flight to Casablanca, waiting for the meal we won't eat, and for the sixteen-ounce Schlitz Malt Liquor beers we would drink, when she pulled out some magazines she had brought. As we were paging through them, one colorful fashion spread captured our attention. It displayed handbags and carry-on luggage made from Turkish kilims. An idea started forming and I realized I could have the same kind of bags made with the Moroccan rugs I had seen in the market. Linda and I talked for hours about all the different styles of bags, from cosmetic bags to overnight bags. She told me what women were looking for in a bag, the types of lining, the closures, whether zippers or snaps—all of that—and how important the straps could be.

As the morning fog lifted off the desert created by the cold ocean currents, Royal Air Maroc's only 747 descended toward the airport, flying very low over a countryside dotted with white adobe farmhouses with flat roofs. This time of day the airport was just opening, so the customs agents, the porters, and the airport security were all jockeying for their positions. We disembarked and boarded some old buses that took us to customs. With only one door open and just a few agents, the line quickly became long and moved slowly.

We observed that some of the passengers didn't wait in line at all and were ushered away where friends and family were waiting. Once we got to the agent, he was surprised to see my other stamp from only a few months before and brought over another official who looked us over and then waved us through. I found a money changer inside the airport who, as before, examined every single hundred-dollar bill up and down, front and back, and I exchanged $500 to dirhams. He told me there were no flights to Marrakech today, and if we still wanted to go, we would have to take the CTM bus to the downtown bus station and wait till the afternoon to catch the bus to Marrakech. The bus was quickly filling up outside the airport entrance, and we were lucky to get the last two remaining seats together. The bus had hot, black vinyl seats and all windows open with the curtains flapping in the wind, indicating no air conditioning. Because the airport was so far out of town, it took us over an hour to get there. Once we arrived at the bus station, the people-watching was boring since there weren't any Berber tribal people or nomadic families, just mostly men in old worn-out wool suits the color of dirt. We quickly fell asleep on a bench with our legs propped up on our luggage, awakening later to a caller shouting, "Marrakech, Marrakech."

The bus was packed with people and all sorts of cargo piled high on the roof. Again, the windows were wide open with flimsy curtains. The bus stopped once for a bathroom break—the men off to one side of a brick wall and the women to the other. It was Linda's first interaction with Moroccan women, as they all squatted together in the squalor. Their djellabas offered them more of a sense of privacy than her blue jeans did. An old plastic water bucket for washing hands was the only "amenity" in this so-called bathroom stop.

Afterward she and I stood around with the other bus riders, stretching our legs, when a man with a monkey on a short rope appeared. We couldn't figure out where he had come from. We didn't see any houses, villages, not even any foot paths leading somewhere. He just appeared. The other passengers and bus driver didn't seem surprised at this; they must have seen him before. He would have the monkey perform tricks for a few coins, breaking up the boredom of the long bus trip.

This man spotted us as foreigners and immediately tried to get Linda to put the monkey on her shoulder, motioning me to take a picture. There was no way she was going to allow this dirty monkey on her shoulder, so when he finally realized it, he moved on to a young Moroccan boy. Once placed on the boy's shoulder, the monkey started shrieking in a high-pitched burst and then turned and bit him on the arm. This created a lot of commotion, with everyone starting to yell at once, so the bus driver decided it would be best if we all got back on the bus. When we looked back through the blowing window curtain, the monkey man was dragging his monkey off to the east, certainly disappointed that there weren't any coins for his pocket that day.

We arrived in Marrakech right as the sun was beginning to set, and disembarked outside the CTM Hotel. I could see Linda's eyes widen as she observed the Square of the Dead for the first time. Any story I had told her could never have prepared her for what her eyes were taking in at that moment. La Hassan came running toward me with a big smile and tried to shake my hand and take my luggage at the same time. We entered the lobby of the hotel, and Omar was there checking in some other guests. "La bes, la bes alec, colshee la bes, hamdula, hamdula." My old room was available, so with La Hassan insisting on carrying all our luggage up the stairs ahead of us, including Linda's woven Kenyan bag with the leather straps around his forehead, we moved into room number 12.

Linda was as excited to see it all as I was to show her, so we changed from our airport clothes and immediately headed back to the square. We wandered from site to site as I told her what I'd seen before. We looked for the black canvas tarp person, and I was relieved when I noticed it in a far corner that night. Suddenly realizing how hungry we were, we decided to eat in my favorite food tent operated by the man with the gold teeth. At that meal, as with all the others in our years to come, Linda was the only woman there. In Moroccan homes the women would stay in the kitchen. Only men went to the restaurants, and Linda would be with me at the round tables seated only with men. If she was ever uncomfortable, she never mentioned it, her brown eyes just observing it all as she and I would talk quietly together.

After finishing our dinner, we walked the square a bit more and then I told her I had a surprise for her. We headed up to the rooftop terrace of the CTM Hotel, where in a far corner I had stashed a bit of hash under a loose brick when I had left months earlier. What we didn't have was any kind of pipe or soup-see, so I impressed her by improvising, putting the small hunk of hash on a safety pin, lighting it, and sticking it under an overturned tea glass. When the glass filled with smoke, we lifted the corner and inhaled deeply. The "spices for the mind" worked their magic, and soon we were ready to leave the terrace and the exotic sights of the square for room number 12 and some good sex and deep sleep.

Linda heard the early morning call to prayer and woke me up, eager to see the sunrise from the terrace. Brecka was already there and as happy to see me as I was to see her and to introduce her to Linda. I asked if she had received the letter I had written her. She smiled up at me with tears in her eyes as she nodded yes. I knew I would feel good about that all day. I then took Linda's hand, guiding her down the narrow stairs on our way to the Café de France and our first kawa halib and croissant.

We were having our second kawa when in walked Ismael. He smiled when he saw me and came to our table. Introductions made, he sat with us for his own breakfast. I knew he wanted to take us both shopping and earn some commissions, but I wasn't interested in having him around as we looked for some rugs and textiles. After coffee I told him we were still tired from the flight and were heading back to our room to rest. Instead, Linda and I circumvented the square, staying out of his line of sight, and walked into the souk a different way.

I had brought over my Moroccan clothes, including the yellow shoes, and was wearing them now, but I needed to buy an outfit for Linda since she felt so conspicuous. As she looked around at the Moroccan women on the street, they were all wearing djellabas made from colorful polyester, but that wasn't her taste. I realized I knew how to help her and took her to Boujma's shop toot-sweet. The birds were outside in their cages as we approached his shop, and his small wooden stool, with what I knew was his soup-see bag underneath, was on the street. We entered, and Boujma was there folding some of his shirts and returning them to their rightful spots in the wooden trunks. He saw me with Linda, who he would eventually love and admire, smiled brightly, and yelled to a young boy to bring us tea. Minutes later the hot tea arrived, and Linda had her first glass of the sweet mint tea that began and ended every day in Morocco. I told Boujma that Linda wanted a nice white Egyptian cotton djellaba, and he, with the same skill he had shown me, opened a trunk and brought out the exact size that would fit her. Linda loved the garment and the quality of the fabric, and slipped it on over her American clothes.

As we were getting ready to leave, Boujma said his neighbor across the alley would like to meet us, and Boujma called him over. He walked across the narrow alley and motioned for Linda to show him her hands. She readily agreed, and he then rubbed a scent on her wrist. The fragrance was intoxicating. He told us this was real musk from the male musk deer. It was priced by weight and sold in small chunks or in metal tins. He asked if we wanted to buy some. Linda loved it, so we crossed the alley into his small shop, which was like a pharmacy that specialized in natural remedies and soaps and scents for the nearby Turkish baths. He took down from a high shelf a large glass jar and scooped out a bit of the musk, weighed it on a primitive metal scale, and wrapped it in a piece of newspaper. He wrote the price on a piece of paper, and I paid him, kissing the last bill. We were ready now to set out for the rug souk. So we bid good-bye to Boujma and his neighbor and were off to see Parisian.

As we were walking to the rug bazaar, I felt like I was back home. Passing through beggar's alley and turning toward the giant archways, I sensed Linda's enthusiasm for all that was ahead, and I knew she would love Marrakech as much as I did.

Parisian was inside his small shop, lying down on a pile of rugs with his Canadian bag nearby. He jumped up, shook my hand—"La bes, la bes alec"—put his arm around my shoulder, and then went to give some coins to a young boy to bring us tea. I couldn't help myself and didn't even wait until the tea had arrived before I began to look through his rugs and weavings. He asked me if I had sold his ten pieces, and I said yes, but when he asked me what I had sold them for, I just smiled and kept silent. I asked Parisian if he had any tightly woven pieces but perhaps with holes in them, thinking of the new bag business. He said he knew where there might be some, but no merchant would have those in his shop. He agreed to try to find me some.

I wanted to take Linda to meet Abdulhey but without telling Parisian because the men were all so competitive with each other. I had learned on my first trip that they each guarded their customers with a fierceness that surprised me, so it was best not to tell anyone who you were dealing with. With the shops so close together in the rug souks, all the owners watched the comings and goings of their neighbors like hungry hawks. There was a great deal of jealousy among them, but it was never spoken about.

Abdulhey wasn't in his shop when we arrived, but the young man who was there remembered me and took off to find Abdulhey and bring us more tea. I could see that Linda was reaching her limit on tea, as I was, but there wasn't any polite way to refuse it.

Abdulhey came bounding into the room with a huge smile and bright eyes, clearly glad to see me. I introduced him to Linda, and we settled in to talk about all that had happened since I left Morocco. Abdulhey was the only person I had met who was modern with his

American clothes and interest in Western culture, and since we both had the same love for the weavings, we were already becoming good friends. I told him about the hitchhiking experience, working at Louie's, and even about wanting to find weavings with the holes in them to start a possible handbag business. He loved hearing everything and said he would try to help me. He mentioned that sometimes those damaged rugs came through the rug auction, adding that we should return that evening.

Linda and I were getting hungry now—the croissants were long gone—so we left to get something to eat. We walked to the Iceberg, where Aziz was waiting with no one there, staring at empty tables, and looked very happy to see me. I ordered my customary shrimp omelet and French fries, but Linda wanted to try the Moroccan food and ordered a chicken and lemon tagine. She loved it, and always being more adventurous than I was with food, the French-Moroccan cuisine was perfect for her.

After lunch we went back to the hotel and rested up to get ready for the rug auction that evening. The auction had already begun as we made our way to Abdulhey's shop. He had the small wood stools already placed near the doorway so we could observe everything. This night there was little of interest for either Abdulhey or me, and I remarked that I was surprised since the night when I had first met Abdulhey with Moktar, there had been so many beautiful rugs. Abdulhey explained that each night of the week had weavings from different areas in Morocco. He said Wednesday evening might be best for the type of weavings I wanted to use for the handbags since that market had rugs from the Khemisset area in the Middle Atlas Mountains. He said it tended to be the biggest auction night of the week. We thanked him and said we would be back in two days to sit with him at that auction.

The next morning I got up early to help Brecka with her wash while Linda slept in. Brecka told me she wanted to give me a henna tattoo to protect me. Later when I told Linda, she wanted one too, so I asked Brecka and she said we should come back in the afternoon after her laundry was done, and she would have everything she needed.

Ismael was waiting for us at the Café de France. I knew I couldn't

keep avoiding him and pretending not to be shopping. After our breakfast I asked Ismael if he knew a place where we could buy things like zippers, needles, thread—items needed for sewing. I was thinking any commission on zippers would not be very much. "Of course," he said, and off we went, following him from the square. We ended up in a narrow alley not even an arm's length wide. On both sides were tiny shops where everything hung randomly. Many women were there buying only one needle or one button. The shops were like those I had seen when buying my yellow shoes, where the merchant sat high up in his shop with his wares all around him. Linda and I began searching for things we might need for our new handbag idea. We found a YKK zipper, thread, scissors, chalk, and needles, and then looked everywhere throughout all the stores we went in until we finally found some D rings to attach the straps.

We left Ismael there, knowing he would collect a little commission from our purchases, and returned to the hotel. Brecka was waiting for us with a small bowl, some lemons, a bag of green powder, and a thin stick. I told her I wanted the tattoo on my back, and she began by mixing the powder with water until it created a paste. She then used the narrow stick and painted the designs on my back. She first made a large square, followed by intricate designs inside the square, and then insisted on putting the henna on my fingernails too. She cut the lemons and squeezed the juice over the paste to help the color deepen, telling me to try not to move much so it would stay in place for a few hours. Brecka drew a traditional design on Linda's hands, one that is drawn on all Moroccan and Berber women before weddings or big events, and painted her fingernails too. When she was finished, she reached into her bag and carefully unwrapped a gift for me. It was a large round crystal about the size of a baseball, held so often with henna-stained hands that the henna had dyed the crystal tips. I could tell by the way she caressed it that this was a rare treasure of hers. I didn't want to accept it, but she insisted.

The next morning we went hunting for some leather skins and leather dye. We decided to go back to where the zippers were and start from there. We wandered past a few more alleys and happened upon an opening where we noticed piles of sheep and goat skins. Men were standing around their individual piles, and it seemed there was an auction on the skins, much like the rug auction. We observed for a while, but the smell was overwhelming, so we picked out a few sheep skins and then asked a young boy about some brown dye. He left for a minute and returned with an oblong chunk of something that looked like hard tar.

We returned to the hotel, and Brecka heated some water for us on her wood stove and dropped the brown dye in it. It took a long time to melt, but when it finally did, we dipped a rag into the dye and rubbed it over the skins, laying them in the sun to dry. We still needed to find some cardboard or something similar to make patterns with, so we headed out again into the souk. Finding any cardboard at all proved to be the biggest challenge because Morocco was basically still a closed country to imports. We finally stumbled upon a refrigerator box behind one of the hotels and returned to the CTM, happy with our successes of the day.

Waiting for that evening's auction, we sat on the terrace of the hotel. I was hard at work on my suntan while trying to keep the flies off me. I had been observing bales of carpets coming in on the buses across the street. Tonight must certainly be the biggest auction of the week, like Abdulhey had told me.

Following the afternoon prayer, Linda and I left the terrace, descended the hotel stairs, and entered the square. We always seemed to attract some young Moroccan guides who would follow us for a while, but by the time we reached Boujma's shop on chicken alley, they disappeared. Maybe it was the medina police up ahead that they saw, or simply Boujma telling them to leave us alone. Whatever the reason, when we reached that alley, we continued alone.

Passing under the arch that led to the carpet bazaar, I could feel a different sort of commotion. The bazaar was jammed with Berber tribesmen, all bringing their treasures to sell. Off to one side I saw a bundle of carpets that had been opened, and they looked like the saddle rugs I had bought before, except larger. The tall man standing there, wearing all white, seemed to know everyone, and everyone stopped to shake his hand and possibly talk about business. Abdulhey saw us standing nearby and motioned for us to come over and sit down. He had tea ready since he had anticipated our coming. He told us that his father would be here soon and was looking forward to seeing me and meeting Linda.

Abdulhey explained how the auction works. The owner of the rug hires a runner who specializes in showing his pieces, and if sold, he will pay him a small percentage. To start the auction, this runner goes to all the merchants in the bazaar who he thinks might be interested in bidding. If he is successful in establishing the opening bid, the carpet is now up for sale.

In the middle of the auction was an open space where the owners and the runners did their business before offering the carpets to the merchants. I quickly realized that the Wednesday market was one I couldn't miss. It was a whirlwind of color and sizes. Among them were long black carpets up to twenty feet long that served as tent walls previously owned by the nomadic people from around the Azrou area. They were coming up for sale because that way of life didn't exist anymore.

All the time the carpets were being thrown to the ground in front of us, Abdulhey seemed to be waiting for something when his father arrived with a man carrying a small bundle under his arm. Haj had a warm smile on his face and told me he was happy to see me again.

I was trying to understand the numbers the people were saying to each other so I could get an idea how much they were selling for. I asked Abdulhey about the prices, and he told me they were all quoted in rials, an old form of Berber money, not dirhams, so that tourists and Moroccans from the cities wouldn't know the real auction price.

After an hour of nonstop activity the tall man dressed in white entered his pieces in the auction. While he was waiting, he came over to greet Haj Medi and Abdulhey and asked if the foreigner had liked any of the pieces, he gave to Haj to show me. Abdulhey then explained to me that he had asked his father to try to find a few good pieces without too many holes or stains so I could cut them up to create handbags. Abdulhey already knew I would like them and told his father's friend that we would buy all four. Haj counted out the money one bill at a time, kissed the last bill, and placed it in the man's outstretched hand.

The auction wound down, with piles of rugs outside most of the merchants' doors. Abdulhey unfolded the weavings his father brought for me. Each one was exactly what I was hoping for. All of them looked similar, the same deep red color, but with different designs. Even though the rugs were made entirely of wool, their weave was as tight as canvas. I asked the price, and Abdulhey said they were not expensive since no one repaired the old pieces, and there was little interest in them now. He asked if around eighty dollars was too much, about twenty dollars each, plus a small commission since that was a way of life here. I glanced at Linda, and she was grinning happily because we had now found all that we had been looking for.

Abdulhey told his father about my idea for the handbag business, and I could see in his face that he was hoping I would become a good customer. Haj asked again if I thought I could sell some of his jewelry, and I again replied, "Enshalah." Then he told me to be sure not to put any of the carpets into my hotel room until I washed them, because they could be full of fleas.

Linda and I couldn't wait to wash the rugs in the morning and begin cutting our patterns. We arrived on the rooftop at the same time Brecka did, eager to get started. We threw them on the old tile, got more savon beldi and scrub brushes, and went to work. While they were drying, we started drawing patterns on our cardboard refrigerator box. We had measured our carry-on bag and had a good idea for one about that size, and Linda had brought a make-up bag that we realized could also be an appropriate size for a woman's purse if we added a shoulder strap.

Once the rugs had dried, we put our chalk and heavy handmade scissors to use, spending the whole day on the rooftop. Linda pulled out the needles we had bought, and the two of us stitched the prototypes together.

At the end of the day we realized that by matching the patterns front to back, we ended up with a lot of waste. So we decided to make a cosmetic bag too, making a complete line.

The next morning we visited Parisian, who had found some pieces with holes that we had asked him for. He also had a few more saddle rugs like those I had bought from him previously. He asked me what I was willing to pay for the weavings with the holes, and I said I had already bought some for 200 dirhams each. He said, "Let's drink tea, and the price will not be a problem, Enshalah."

We settled in for tea, and Parisian started showing us other weavings. Some we had not seen before—white sequined wedding blankets from an area called Zaine, where the women were supposedly the most beautiful women of the High Atlas and were heavily tattooed on their faces, upper chests, and inner thighs. We had already learned about the tattoos on these women. Some were for protection from the evil eye, but others were a brand to show what village or tribe they were from in case they were kidnapped.

We left Parisian's shop with a bundle of cut-ups and a few of the white sequined wedding blankets. The next day we were back on the rooftop with Brecka, washing our new acquisitions and cutting patterns from the ones cleaned the day before.

That afternoon, about the time that the market started, we took our samples and the patterns we had cut to Abdulhey. He was as excited as we were, and he immediately wanted to introduce us to a friend of his, Abdulhuck, who he had gone to the university with. Abdulhuck had several sewing machines and a lot of relatives who worked for him and his leather bag business. Abdulhuck understood the patterns we showed him, plus the samples we had sewn. We handed him the leather skins, the zippers, the D rings, and all else, and hoped we would be happy when we arrived back in a few days.

From the rooftop terrace the next morning I located the entryway to the fonduk Moktar had taken me to, and I wanted to show Linda what I had experienced. She and I went there after early morning kawa halib at Café de France because when Moktar and I had arrived before in the afternoon, the merchants were so busy buying that there wasn't any room for us. On that first visit men were lined up with plastic gym bags filled with amber, amazonite, even snake skins, to sell to the merchants. In the afternoon the merchants weren't interested in selling, only in buying. As we walked up the narrow stairwell, we took a deep breath to get past the stinky bathroom and keep moving upward.

Bashir had the closest store to the stairwell, and he greeted us with a bright smile and a welcoming look. We didn't mention Moktar or Ben Ali because it didn't seem necessary, and with what we had learned about the Moroccan commission business, it seemed best to keep it a secret. Bashir was charming and dressed like a person from the Sahara with his indigo robe and silver cross around his neck. He had prayer scars on his forehead between his eyes, and henna hands. He was so open and welcoming, we immediately felt at home. In his shop Bashir offered silver, coral, amber, silver daggers, and artifacts from the south, and to me he looked like someone who could have been a movie star. He served a different type of tea, with a more elaborate process, and the more time we spent, the more willing Bashir was to show us items of more value from the lower drawers of his desk.

I had been so enthralled with the textiles, I hadn't even thought about the jewelry that Morocco had to offer. Haj Midi had tempted me for sure, but up until that morning with Bashir, I hadn't really considered investing any money in Berber jewelry. Now, Linda and I were looking at all of this—she, picking out a ring or two for herself, and I, searching for the silver bracelet I'd always wanted. I found one and was told it was a slave's bracelet from the south in a style called neillo—silver etching on brass—that fastened with a small screw.

After another wonderful hour with Bashir, we heard the call for afternoon prayers and said our good-byes. But before we left, we asked Bashir if there was anything he would like from the States, and he too said he wanted a letter or a postcard.

In the far corner of the fonduk we noticed what we believed was antique terra-cotta pottery with similar designs to what were displayed on the carpets, and I suspected they were used for olive oil and olive storage.

The following morning we woke up ready to see the handbags that Abdulhuck had made. They were not double stitched as we had requested, and the leather for the strap was not folded over, so it had a raw edge. He had also forgotten to include a pocket inside. We understood it was the first attempt and told him to start over, but now we had lost the rug. At the end of Abdulhuck's alley were three older men sitting up in their stalls, using their toes to hold a T bar where they were braiding a strap that we had seen as those used for daggers. We bought a few of them, thinking they might work for our handbag strap.

We decided to take a taxi to the French quarter in Guilez for the afternoon. I was interested in finding any books on carpets or pottery, and perhaps even the French photographer's book that Ben Ali had about Berber women. Walking the streets, we came across a camera store selling not only film but also the books I wanted. We discovered six black-and-white photographs of Berber women and the book I had perused at Ben Ali's.

Time for dinner, and happy with our purchases, we searched for a restaurant. Luckily, we passed an old hotel that had seen bad times, and hanging from a fig tree nearby was a newly painted sign with an arrow directing us to the Rotisserie restaurant. Up ahead we could see tables with umbrellas on the street. It could have been in the movie *Casablanca*, with dining around a fountain in the summer and near the indoor fireplace in the winter. The Rotisserie became our favorite restaurant for many years.

The next morning we cut up more patterns from Parisian's pieces and delivered them to Abdulhuck that evening for him to try again. We then headed to one of the small spice shops, where they displayed miniature turtles in cages outside their door, along with hanging snake skins, an assortment of dried reptiles, bird feathers, and plastic jars filled with assorted spices and herbal remedies. We bought some frankincense, amber, and musk, leaving with strong smells on our arms because every piece had been rubbed into our wrists by the shopkeeper.

Our next grouping of bags from Abdulhuck were perfect, and we asked him to hire a few more friends or relatives so we could have more bags produced in a shorter period of time. He offered to buy the leather skins and dye them for us, saying he could get a better price and quality, so we stopped doing this ourselves. A few days later we had twenty-five bags, some of all three styles. We decided to mail them to the States so we would have our luggage free for the rugs and textiles we were buying.

There were two post offices in Marrakech, one for mailing letters and buying stamps, which was right around the corner from the CTM Hotel and directly across from the Club Med. The other post office was about a mile away down Mohammed V Boulevard, close to the French outdoor vegetable market. They also accepted letters and sold stamps, but their main purpose was for shipping packages and parcels internationally. You had to go around to the back to get your merchandise packed, inspected, and shipped.

They would allow you to ship only one parcel a day, and the weight limit was ten kilos. Just one man for the entire post office had the job of sorting and packing your merchandise for you. He used his own packing tape, homemade scissors, brown paper, and string.

Once the customs inspector searched your items, the other man would then wrap them in brown paper and tie them with string. It was customary to tip him so your items were packed well and nothing was missing. I made a mental note to return with gifts for him on my next trip from the States, like new lightweight scissors, a utility knife, and some 3M packing tape. To save money I would walk to the post office in the early morning before it got too hot. It normally took about three or four weeks for my packages to arrive in the States, they told me, and somehow they always arrived intact and mostly on time.

Even though Abdulhuck had hired more relatives, we still were not getting enough handbags and luggage made before our departure date from Morocco. We decided to talk to Parisian to see if he would help us. He had proved invaluable in finding us a lot of the cut-up rugs, and because it was the Moroccan way, once we told him we were paying 200 dirhams each, he sold them to us for 180 to hurt his competition.

We found Parisian outside his shop, watching the market and sitting on his little stool. We had brought with us a few of the finished bags Abdulhuck had made to show him what we needed. We told him we wanted to find other people who could sew the bags for us and asked if he knew anyone. Of course, he replied, saying his brother's friend Abslem had his own machine and could help us. Parisian also advised us to keep this a big secret because anyone else who sees the bags will immediately start copying them, and when we return to Marrakech, they will be all over the market. "This is a country of thieves," he told us. We agreed to meet at his shop the next day, and he would bring Abslem so we could show him the bags.

That night when Linda and I were eating dinner at the Iceberg, we started discussing what Parisian had said about our idea being copied. We had already seen how the souks all carried the same things, and how they were all near to each other. We had joked and called it "safety in numbers," but that was before we had an idea we wanted kept secret. It would be hard to keep a secret in the souk.

As much as we liked Abdulhuck, we realized that with his sewing machines being visible in his shop, and with the activity of people coming and going looking for leather jackets and leather bags, it would not take long for someone to see what he was making for us and want to buy them, and before long Abdulhuck would start making and selling them in his shop. Parisian was right; everyone was looking to do something different, and when something different turned out to be profitable, everyone started duplicating it.

The next morning we arrived at Parisian's shop, and already sitting with him having tea was a very small Berber man who Parisian said lived outside the city on the way to the airport. Abslem didn't speak any English, but we could see that he understood the bags and the patterns we brought for him to cut. We wanted to have Abslem and Parisian cut the patterns, buy and dye the leather skins, and make the bags ready to ship. We also showed them the hand-braided dagger straps the three old men made and mentioned we wanted these for the straps. We told them about making the small cosmetic bag with the leftover pieces of carpet. We explained everything repeatedly, with "Enshalah" being said by all of us. We also learned another Arabic word, pronounced *arfte*, meaning "I understand." When Parisian felt we were explaining the whole process too many times, he would say this to us, sounding a bit exasperated. We left Abslem and Parisian with our fingers crossed, hoping we would be happy with the bags when we returned in a few days. Enshalah.

Two days later we met Parisian and Abslem, and the finished product with the dagger strap was waiting for us to approve. We were delighted with their work. Abslem had done a nice job wrapping the black cotton lining around the inside seams, and all the stitching was correct. Linda and I liked the idea that the bags were being made at Abslem's home by the airport, away from any wandering eyes. We negotiated prices, and I talked to Parisian about shipping them directly to us in the States if I telephoned him to say that we needed them. He remembered shipping the wallets to Canada through the post and agreed. I reminded him about how he had cheated the Canadian by only making a few good wallets and how he then had lost the man's business, and told him it would happen to him again if he was not smarter. "Arfte, arfte," he replied.

We were so happy after our success with Parisian, we decided to go back to the CTM Hotel and toast our success in a special way. We had found a djellaba at the market earlier, which was made from a woven wool so light and fine it was transparent and called *bizouey*, the cloth of the kings. It fit Linda perfectly, and she came out of the bathroom with it on, and nothing underneath. We lit our frankincense and a candle, and the magic that is Marrakech took over.

We were talking later, on the rooftop again, observing the spectacle below us on the square. The black tarp person was now dead center in the middle. Linda and I were mentioning how we couldn't believe all our good fortune, how everything seemed to be falling into place, and how she sensed, as I did on my first trip, that perhaps she had been here before. It all was so different, yet so comfortable.

Linda and I decided to attend the auction the next night. How quickly a week had gone by; it was already Wednesday. We walked into Abdulhey's shop and saw him speaking with his father. Both men greeted us with large smiles, ordered us tea, and placed the wooden stools by the entrance to the shop so we could observe the auction that was about to begin. Linda always sat on the stool farthest from the doorway, Haj closest to the door, and Abdulhey and I together so he could talk to me about everything.

We noticed the same man we had seen last week, again dressed all in white, standing on the side with a large bundle opened near him. He motioned to Abdulhey to come over and see what he had brought. The Moroccan hand motion for "come" is the Western up-and-down motion for good-bye. Abdulhey grabbed my hand and took me with him. The first thing I observed was a long, narrow, tightly woven sash or belt that I had seen the Berber women wearing in Bertrand's photography book. He also had some weavings that we were told were handerias, which women wear like shawls. Quickly folding them up before anyone else could see them, Abdulhey told the man to follow him back to the shop. We agreed on a price, again with Abdulhey telling me this was the price plus some commission, and I bought all the pieces.

We returned to the hotel, realizing that our duffle bags for the trip home were almost full, but that was OK because we were leaving in a few days anyway.

On our last day we went into the souk to say our good-byes. Taking a different route in, about halfway down a narrow street, we stopped and realized we were in an area where there weren't any shops—not a tourist area, just residential homes. Linda and I both had a moment of feeling we had been there before, although we never had.

We started with Boujma and asked him our standard question: "Is there anything we can bring you from the States?" Instead of a postcard or letter, he asked for some cotton men's underwear, and perhaps a bottle of Scotch. Enshalah. Every trip for years I would bring him the underwear and Scotch, until one of his neighbors told me not to bring the Scotch anymore. He said Boujma would take the bottle, drink it all in a day, and not open his shop for a few days. He added that I was killing my friend. After that, he got only the underwear.

We then entered the rug souk to say our good-byes to our friends there. Linda and I had talked about wanting to make it quick since we didn't have any more money and were always tempted by the treasures there. And our teeth were hurting from all the sweet mint tea we couldn't refuse without being rude. We collected business cards with addresses and planned to send everyone a postcard from the States. We got out within an hour, a new record for us.

Linda and I passed through customs separately at JFK, each with our big bags. Both of us got waved through this time, so we celebrated with a cold Heineken beer, toasting our first trip together to Marrakech

Chapter Six

Santa Fe and Sugar

◇◇

Back in Brownsville, after a delicious filet steak dinner, we were showing Linda's parents all the things we had bought, and Paul said to Betty, "Let's have a cocktail party, and T.R. can show these weavings to our friends and see if any of them want to buy anything." Paul seemed to get a big kick out of doing this and, on the night of the cocktail party, showed up with a box of business cards he had made for me. The only words were "T.R. Lawrence – Importer." Our post shipment of the handbags came in just in time for the party, and we were ready.

The cocktail party was a big success, and it showed us that designing purses was a good business, and that many women would buy one. Paul and Betty bought a few things for their home, and a couple of their friends did too. One of them had a summer home in Estes Park, Colorado, where I knew the wool weavings would look spectacular. Another guest at the cocktail party mentioned the Dallas trade shows and suggested we go there and try to find a rep for our handbag line. So off we went.

The Dallas Trade Mart was confusing and difficult to navigate. It was strictly a wholesale show; only store owners or people with business licenses were allowed to sell. We walked up and down the aisles with the handbags thrown over our shoulders. A few of the showroom owners and manufacturer reps became interested in what we showed them. After having done business in the bazaar of Marrakech, my senses were highly intuitive, and I didn't get a good feeling about them, so Linda and I kept walking the halls.

#901
Barrel Purse. One of our top sellers.

ILLUSTRATED BY CHRISTOPHER MAYES

We ended up on the second floor, by the down escalator, which was a great location, and saw a showroom with the name Leon Goetz on the door. We entered and showed Leon the bags. He loved them and was unbelievably charming. This time I did have a good feeling. We talked about the bag business and hired him as our rep. Leon told us about a gift show in a few weeks and invited us to work the showroom with him.

Back at the island we cleared another shipment through customs and spent the next few days sewing in labels that said "100% wool, handmade in Morocco." We also came up with the name for our business: Nomads. Renting a van for the weekend of the Dallas gift show, we arrived the day before the market opened. The day of our first market Linda and I dressed to kill and joined Leon, his mother, and his staff. Leon's mother was as charming as he was. They were from Louisiana and both had that southern accent and style. Leon had offered us the front window for our display, and we were completely overwhelmed at the interest in our handbags. People stood in line waiting for us to take their order.

On the first day we met Roger Horchow from the Horchow catalog, and the buyer from Neiman Marcus. They each placed orders with us, among many other store owners from around the States. We noticed that several stores in Santa Fe, New Mexico, had placed large orders, and Leon insisted that we go there and show the rugs we had.

Leon had also invited Alex, a gentleman with estate jewelry, to sell at his booth, so in the off time, normally around lunch, we would chat with him. He was intriguing and told us about the diamond business in New York. At the end of the market I told Linda to pick out a ring from Alex to celebrate our success.

On the drive back Linda added up all the orders on a calculator and figured out how many of each style we would need. I tried to get ahold of Parisian to tell him, but never could. This was years before the internet or fax machines, so I finally sent a telegraph and asked him to call me. He never did, but a week later I got a telegraph from him saying, "No you in phone."

Linda and I were on the road to Santa Fe within a week, with the orders and other things we had brought from Morocco. I would never forget the first time driving down Old Pecos Trail—the small, old adobe homes lining the street, with the mountains in the background.

As we walked around town, looking for the businesses that had ordered the handbags, I was thinking how much Santa Fe resembled Marrakech. The store owners were happy that we had hand-delivered the bags and asked what else we had. We showed our rugs, and they bought all that we had carried with us.

We decided to stay a few more days and soon realized that Santa Fe not only reminded us of Marrakech, but was talking to us like Marrakech had. We couldn't stay on the island and do business, and Santa Fe seemed to be the right spot. The Moorish-Spanish influence, plus the size of the city, was so appealing. No highways to navigate, no ugly strip malls to spoil the view. We noticed a store on our first day named Seret and Sons, which had architectural items of antique doors, windows, trunks, and masses of rugs—all mainly from India and Afghanistan. I thought this could be us, except from Morocco. All the people we had met so far in Santa Fe were incredibly interesting. Santa Fe was beginning to get a lot of publicity then—although it had always been a tourist market for the Texans escaping the summer heat—now the rest of the country was learning about it too. Ralph Lauren had just released a whole Southwest look—concha belts, denim skirts, and Native American textile-pattern sweaters.

We wandered around and found a location on a small side street named Shelby that was around the corner from Seret's. Once again we took a giant leap and signed a one-year lease with options. Now we needed to find a place to live. That proved to be more difficult since Santa Fe was just beginning to boom and the housing shortage was acute. We found one place near Canyon Road, but the landlady said she didn't want to rent it to us because a movie star had looked at it first and *might* decide to rent it. We even offered her more money, but it didn't matter—she was starstruck.

We left a $1,000 deposit with a real estate agent, telling him to just find some place for us to live, and headed off to Marrakech a few weeks later.

We checked again into the CTM Hotel and got our old room back. We were happy to see everyone again, including Brecka, who had received our second postcard. Seeing her reminded us that our henna tattoos had already faded. That night, with the sounds of the alley cats fighting and the beggars praying to God under a full moon, we ascended to the terrace. As we were listening to the calls of the snake charmers in the square, we gazed at each other and felt we were falling even more in love.

The next morning, after the second call to prayer, we headed off to see Parisian. Our long-distance communication had been inadequate, so we were curious to see what handbags he and Abslem had made. Parisian had created a lot of stock, and each bag was flawless. We were thrilled, and at his request I paid him with U.S. dollars, not dirhams. He mentioned that some of his friends were going to Mecca and needed U.S. dollars. That kind of exchange would be something we would do for years to come. Apparently, to travel to Mecca the only currency any pilgrim wanted was the U.S. dollar, and new greenbacks at that.

We left Parisian's shop delighted, and we had given him the Horchow order and all other orders to get busy with. We then decided to visit some of our other friends to purchase things for our new store. We went to Boujma with his selection of clothes, Bashir in the fonduk with his artifacts and Berber jewelry, Yousef with his antiques, Abdulhey with his weavings, and his father, Haj, with the jewelry pieces.

We bought Boujma's bottle of Scotch from the duty-free shop, which we brought to him wrapped in newspaper and hidden in a bag with the underwear in a guffa straw basket with large handles. Boujma greatly appreciated the Scotch and underwear and said, "Please sit awhile and have tea and a soup-see." While his parrots made noises overhead, I said, "*Allish-alah*," meaning "why not?" We always had time for Boujma. We decided to order the men's Egyptian cotton shirts with the Nehru collars—what I was then wearing—in multiple sizes for our new store, with a few women's embroidered felt jackets as well.

From Boujma's shop we meandered our way to the fonduk to see Bashir. We asked if he had received our postcard of the skyline of Dallas, and he motioned to where it was taped to the wall behind him. Bashir invited us to his home the next day, and we were not sure if it was because of the postcard, or because we were opening a store in Santa Fe and were planning to do a lot of business with him. Bashir picked us up with a horse-drawn carriage outside of the CTM Hotel, the same kind I had taken from the airport with Ben Ali. We went through the Jewish quarter, past the Bahia Palace to the outskirts of town. As we got closer to what we assumed was our destination, women and children waved hello to us, without head scarves or fear of foreigners.

We stepped down from the carriage and were surrounded by Bashir's family members, tribal elders, and neighbors. We were an anomaly; everyone wanted to touch us, touch our hair, look into my blue eyes, and the women couldn't wait to grab Linda and take her into a back room. Once in that room, they peeled off her head scarf, and someone started combing her hair as another relative began lining her eyes with kohl and putting organic rouge on her cheeks and lips. For a fair Irish-Swedish girl from Minnesota, this was far too exotic, and I had to smile.

The women in Bashir's family were incredibly beautiful with dark hair and blue eyes, a little like Haj Midi. While Linda was being made over and given the highest honor the women could offer, I was on the rooftop being shown museum-quality artifacts from Bashir's own collection. He explained that this would help educate my eye.

Linda and I had a memorable afternoon there, with many courses of wonderful food, as is the Moroccan way, but this had a Sub-Saharan twist. Hours later Bashir drove us in the carriage back to our hotel. Linda had so much makeup on, and it was so garish on her light skin, that she felt totally conspicuous in the carriage, but she also knew this had been an experience of a lifetime. We stopped at the CTM Hotel so Linda could wash off all the makeup before we set out into the souk following the afternoon prayer.

I wanted to drop in on Yousef, the man I had met with Moktar who had bought the antique samovar I admired. Finding his small shop, Linda and I entered. Yousef got up, not quite sure if he recognized me, and asked us to sit as he got us tea. He then asked me if I knew Moktar, Ben Ali Karbush's uncle. I said, "Yes, I was here before with Moktar," adding that I had enjoyed looking around his shop, and that we wished to do so again. "Merhabban," he said.He then showed Linda and me some of his beautiful Berber necklaces made with amber, coral, and antique silver amulets. Yousef took the time to educate us about amber. What were commonly called amber beads in the market were actually resin beads made in France over a hundred years ago. The term for real amber in Morocco was *lubin*, and Yousef said we should always ask for lubin if we wanted to buy the real beads made from the petrified pine sap that is the true amber.

Yousef's gallery was beautiful; his well-illuminated glass cases lined the walls and made everything look valuable. I could see why Karbush had been buying and trading with him and his father for years. He enticed us to buy a few of his Berber necklaces for our new store. Yousef also displayed some antique wooden containers that had been used to store the kohl eye makeup for the women in the mountains. They were small hand-carved sculptures, each with a thin stick applicator that was part of the lid. Some of them had the appearance of tiny castles or mosques, intricately carved, and some were painted with what we assumed must be plant or insect dyes. The containers also had an exotic smell. Linda and I found these miniature carved containers so beautiful, we bought a small collection, thinking no one had ever seen these in Santa Fe.

Leaving Yousef's shop, we wandered back into the rug souk, still searching for more rugs to cut up for the handbags. We had learned all the entrances and exits to this area of the souk since we often needed to evade someone who wanted us to buy something that didn't match our taste. If we simply avoided the alley where their shop was, and they didn't see us coming and going, there weren't any hurt feelings. That afternoon we were entering by the pigeon-and-rabbit alley when we heard the familiar Moroccan hiss. We saw two tall, thin young men—obviously brothers—in a tiny shop tucked in a corner we hadn't noticed before.

Word was already out in the market that we were searching for old, thin weavings with holes in them. We entered their dark shop, and they began showing us several red pieces perfect for the handbags. I had learned to say right from the start that I wanted a serious price, that I wasn't interested in bargaining and blah blah blah. Everyone seemed to understand this, and most of the time they would give me a wholesale price or close to it right away, knowing I would pay cash on the spot, saving us all a lot of time.

I always carried an invoice book that made two copies, and wrote down what we paid. It came in handy with new merchants since we could show them we bought this particular piece from Abdulhey or Parisian and paid this or that price. I would write it down and give everyone a copy, though we were certain most of the men couldn't read it, except for the numbers. Word was also out that we didn't ask for credit or consignment, even though it was always offered. If the dealers were hungry that day or hadn't made a sale in a while, it worked to our advantage.

That evening the brothers went out of their way to show us twenty pieces that were already cleaned and ready to be cut up. We bought them all. They called for a carosa and paid the driver to deliver them to the CTM Hotel. I already knew from experience that I would have to pay the carosa driver again once he arrived at the hotel. The drivers would always want more, and it became an argument. Yet what else

could I expect from a poor man who had no family and lived and slept in a pushcart in an alley?

Even though we had asked Parisian and Abslem to cut and wash the weavings, we wanted to speed up the production and get more stock quicker. I began to wake up early to help Brecka, and then wash and cut my own patterns and drop them off at Parisian's shop in the afternoon. The Moroccan handmade scissors were an instrument of torture, so I wrapped rags through the handles just to be able to cut through the weavings without too many blisters. One of the other big issues for our bag business was finding brown zippers. We had already exhausted every shop that sold the YKK brand, which produced stronger and better zippers—the only ones we would settle for. One enterprising store owner boarded the bus to Casablanca and brought us back a bundle. Finding the hand-braided dagger straps was also problematic. The three men at the end of Abdulhuck's alley were the only ones who still knew how to braid the dagger straps. They were old men and didn't like to work that hard, so it was always a challenge getting the straps we needed.

Most evenings after dinner Linda and I would wander through the Square of the Dead and check out the action. The snake charmers no longer bothered us by trying to get us to hold their snakes for a photograph at a price. We were recognized by then as ones who knew their way around. We would shop the different blankets where people put their items up for sale—old brass trays, white metal teapots, carved hammers used for breaking up sugar, leather camel cushions from the Sahara, a mixture of new and old, good stuff and junk, all randomly displayed on dirty blankets.

We convinced Parisian to learn about ocean container shipping. So far we had only been making air freight shipments and using the post. We wanted our business to grow, but couldn't export the quantity of items we would need to expand it without shipping the merchandise in containers. To add variety to our inventory, we also wanted antique pottery and old Moroccan doors and windows. Parisian had a source for them and other items. We began buying some beautiful painted furniture pieces, wedding trunks, small shelves, inlaid bone trunks and mirrors, even things like donkey baskets from the Ourika Valley.

We discovered that no one had ever shipped an ocean container of artisanal merchandise from Marrakech before, and we were going to be the first. I found out the container would come by train from Casablanca to Marrakech, where we would fill it, then it would go back to Casablanca on the train to the seaport, where it would be put on a ship to Rotterdam, Holland, then transferred to another container ship bound for Houston, Texas, and finally trucked to Santa Fe. I also learned we needed a different shipping license for ocean containers because it required more governmental paperwork.

Within a few days Parisian introduced us to Omar, the director of the artisan exports from Marrakech, and Parisian had rented a small warehouse to help us store our many new acquisitions. Omar was only interested to know what we were planning to ship in the containers, so we agreed to show him everything in the warehouse before loading each container. Omar had brought the necessary paperwork and stamps with him, so it seemed so easy. I paid him one-hundred dirhams as he left, and he instructed me to take the papers to the customs office in Guilez. The customs office was easy to find, but no one seemed friendly. I showed them all the paperwork from Omar, and they told me I needed additional forms before they would release the container. I went to Omar, got the additional forms, a few more stamps, and paid another one-hundred dirhams. This became routine, and for six days I repeated the process, each day realizing I needed an additional form. On the seventh day the customs official said everything was in order and stamped my papers for the container. The next time I saw Omar, I said I wanted to just give him the 700 dirhams at once for all the paperwork, and he thought that was an excellent idea.

Getting our merchandise from the warehouse in Bab Dukala to the train station was a challenge. Parisian and I hired a man who owned four horse-drawn wagons and could supply us with six workers. He was willing to do this for us in the middle of the night because there was too much traffic during the day. The men and wagons arrived at three in the morning, and they silently packed and carried everything on their shoulders to the wagons. We had hired men like this before, and we nicknamed them "the men with no zippers." Living on the streets, they wore every item of clothing they owned, and invariably the last pair of pants on top of the other pair of pants was always missing a zipper.

No one was on the streets this early in the morning, only a few old men going to the mosque after the first call to prayer in the gray period of the dawn. We had been told that this first prayer was the most auspicious because you had the chance of getting your prayers answered before all the million other people prayed for their own wants and needs. Finally, everything was strapped down and the horses and drivers were ready to go. I decided to ride with the oldest of the drivers, thinking he might be safer. Linda watched as the men stood upright in their wooden wagons and cracked their whips over the heads of their black stallions, and we left in the dark of night toward the train station.

We got to the station and located the container sitting on some nineteenth-century railroad tracks all by itself near the customs office. The container was at least fifty yards away from the closest spot we could bring our wagons, making it impossible to pack. The man wanted his wagons back, so we had to unload all the merchandise onto the dirt. Parisian and I tried to get the conductor of the train to move the container closer to the merchandise, and we had a standoff with him for two days. The conductor kept wanting more "sugar," as he called it. Finally, we had satisfied him with enough tips that he agreed to move it. I kissed our first container as it left the railroad station and thanked both God and Allah for helping me with this.

With only a few more days before our departure from Morocco, and not enough money left for shopping, we took a side trip and got out of Marrakech for our remaining time. We had heard a lot about Essaouira, originally a fishing village on the Atlantic Ocean named Mogador. We were told that the wind always blew off the ocean. It wasn't a place for a beach vacation, but years later when wind surfing became popular, Essaouira became a desired destination for that sport. When we arrived on our first trip, there were few tourists, and everyone left us alone. After the hustle and bustle of Marrakech, it was a welcome reprieve.

We stayed at a hotel facing the ocean and discovered only one restaurant, Chez Sam, across from the hotel on the wharf. The owner had two German shepherds that wandered around the tables, looking for scraps. All the homes in this picturesque city were painted white with blue rooftops and trim, like those on the islands in Greece. The women were draped in long white fabric, which they wrapped around themselves, showing only their eyes, and at sunset they would walk the seawall in groups of two or three.

The city itself was surrounded by old ramparts built by the Portuguese, with ancient cannons still present. The fishing area was the most interesting to us—a mass of ropes and nets, skeletons of old wooden boats, fishermen with their day's catch in baskets, and a shipyard where they built by hand the wooden fishing trawlers designed to tackle the rough North Atlantic seas. In the late afternoon we observed poor women coming to the docks, and the fishermen would give them the unsold, leftover pilot fish, otherwise known as eels, which they wrapped in newspaper and took home.

We slept late, ate a lot of fish, and wandered the town lazily. Without any souks like those in Marrakech, the city offered nothing that tempted us to spend money. But it was romantic and we were in love, so our vacation was wonderful. After a few days we traveled back to Marrakech to finish our business, pack our bags, and prepare for the next chapter of our life.

❧ Chapter Seven ❧

Seeing New Possibilities

◇◇◇◇◇◇◇◇◇◇◇◇◇◇◇◇◇◇◇◇◇◇◇◇◇◇◇◇

THE REAL ESTATE AGENT in Santa Fe had found us a new two-bedroom condo off West Houghton Street about ten blocks from our new store. It was newly constructed with a kiva fireplace, all new appliances, and a small outside enclosed area for our dog, Nomad. It felt perfect, especially after the old beach house we had been living in.

That first container arrived in Santa Fe safe and sound about six weeks later, and we were thrilled with all the new merchandise for our new life. Somehow or another we got everything done. We worked like dogs, painted the new store, hung display racks, found antique jewelry cases, and opened our retail store in Santa Fe on May 1. We were exhausted yet enthusiastic about what this new life would bring for us.

Besides Seret's store around the corner, there was a famous Santa Fe restaurant named Periscope on our street. Unbeknown to us it had a large following. On our very first day a woman walked in, pointed to a shelf with six green pieces of antique pottery, and said, "I want to buy them all." I looked at her in disbelief. "You haven't even looked at them yet or asked the price," and she replied that she had seen them on her way to the restaurant the night before and that the price didn't matter. Linda and I glanced at each other and knew what we were both thinking: *Boy, do we love this place!*

A few months after we opened Nomads, a well-dressed man came in one afternoon who loved the textiles and jewelry we had on display. He introduced himself as Doug Walton, and said he was an artist from Ruston, Louisiana. As Linda and I shared stories of Morocco with him, he asked if we would consider conducting tours to Marrakech. Linda and I had never considered it before, but we thought, *Allish-alah*—why not?

Doug mentioned that not only was he a well-known artist, he also taught watercolor painting and had a following of mainly women who would attend his workshops in Ruston. He was interested in branching out to other places for the workshops, and when he met us, it all seemed to fall into place.

By the end of the day we had chosen a date about six months later for our first tour. Doug would supply the people and do the morning watercolor instruction, and I was to handle the rest. Linda and I started thinking about all the adventures we could share. Once Doug sent us the list of the artists who had signed up, and their addresses, we mailed a letter with a questionnaire to each of them, asking for their favorite colors and clothing size. Included was a list of Moroccan words for them to practice, and hopefully learn, and we suggested they bring some used clothing for the poor and some hard candies for the beggar children to make their trip more memorable. Being young and enthusiastic, I researched how to buy group airline tickets on Royal Air Maroc and became my own travel agent. I was rewarded with one free round-trip ticket.

With the six-month deadline for the tour, we decided that I should return to Morocco and figure out the logistics for the group. Linda needed to stay in Santa Fe, fill the handbag orders that were still coming in from the Dallas showroom, and run the retail store that had gotten busier because of the good publicity we were receiving.

I followed my travel routine: book my ticket on Royal Air Maroc with my favorite seat, 56K, get to JFK, and then on to Casablanca, Marrakech, and the CTM Hotel. When I checked in, I asked Omar if it was possible to take a bus to Khemisset Village Market, and he said that the bus would get me there too late for the market and that

I needed to catch a taxi by the police station. The next morning I was eager to go, so I got up around 4:30 a.m. before the call to prayer, dressed quickly in my Moroccan clothes and yellow shoes, sporting a new mustache, and headed to the taxi stand. I negotiated and was willing to pay more so I could get the front seat by myself, while four Berber men crammed into the back seat. Still dark out, we all fell asleep. When the sun came up, the taxi driver pulled over to a roadside café about halfway between Khemisset and Marrakech. Without ordering, we were served bread, olive oil, argan oil, and hot mint tea. We finished quickly because we were interested in getting to the market before it opened.

Now that the sun was up, I saw out the passenger window some black tents on the horizon, too far away for photographs or for tourists to visit. Some goats and sheep were being herded along the road by a second or third son. It had been explained to me that only the first son was in line for any inheritance, so the second or third son would become the goat or sheep herders.

As we approached the village of Khemisset, people on both sides of the road were headed in the same direction, some in horse-drawn wagons loaded with things for sale, some on horseback, some leading donkeys or mules for sale. Sharing the road with us were taxis with buyers like me looking for treasures. The market was on the outskirts of town, and it opened every week on Wednesday. After the taxi driver dropped us off, I asked him to wait.

I wandered the market, and I was on my own. Even with my Moroccan disguise people could easily spot me as a foreigner, yet I was not afraid. It appeared that everything was available for sale: vegetables, animals, spices and seeds, and the services of village doctors and barbers. I just kept walking and observing and ended up in an area behind an adobe wall where I noticed what I thought were newly made rugs, folded to look like pyramids, with a man standing next to them offering them for sale. Off to the left under some cedar trees a group of men sat among piles of antique carpets. I recognized one of them as having been in the back seat of my taxi, and perhaps from the Berber market in Marrakech.

I approached, hesitating slightly, took a few deep breaths, and joined the group. I offered my hand to the man in the taxi, and he accepted it. I told him my name was Lawrence, and he said his was Omar. I sifted through the piles of rugs on the ground, and I was interested in buying a few of them, but my passion was still pushing me to find the saddle rugs like those I had bought from Parisian. Placing a few of the weavings to the side near Omar, I negotiated a fair price and paid him, and then asked if anyone had any of the saddle rugs. Omar said there was a man from Tiflit named Boukar who had been collecting old weavings for years, ever since he was a young man. He was once a wood cutter in the mountains and had seen the weavings drying on the old adobe walls in the remote Kasbahs. Omar offered to take me to meet him at his small shop in the market, but since I understood the commission system, I asked him for directions instead. Omar grudgingly agreed and told me to look for a white tent by the main entrance. I left the weavings I had purchased and asked the men to watch them while I went to meet Boukar.

I located a small white tent, entered it, and immediately saw the splendor I had been dreaming of. Boukar spoke no English, so I went through his stack of weavings and found a few fabulous saddle rugs. I already knew what the prices should be, but since he gave me the prices in rials on small pieces of paper, my negotiations took longer than normal. He then showed me some different rugs that excited me. Coming from the same area as the finely woven saddle rugs were also pile rugs that were black with red designs and woven in mohair and camel wool. They were thick and so soft, and I learned that most of the larger ones were used for bedding. These marvelous weavings prompted me to imagine the man who had owned these carpets and slept on them, and the women in his family who wove them. I felt anew that Morocco was speaking to me.

After a few hours and glasses of mint tea, I had a nice collection of rugs and weavings from Boukar, plus the ones from Omar, to take back to Marrakech. The taxi wasn't large enough to accommodate them, so Omar mentioned that the CTM bus now in town could take my bundles to Marrakech after it went on its circuitous route to Casablanca and back south again. I rolled them all up in the four duffle bags I had brought with me, and the driver threw them on the racks on the top of the bus and handed me a small slip of paper with numbers on it that I didn't understand. I prayed it wouldn't rain. I got in a different taxi with different men, but this time I couldn't sit in the front passenger seat. I had stayed too long and this was the last taxi driving back to Marrakech. I arrived at the CTM Hotel many hours later, exhausted but happy to have experienced this village market and to have learned more about the business.

The next day was Thursday, and I needed to put my attention on Doug Walton's art workshops. I had to find a nice hotel for the group, and the CTM Hotel wouldn't meet those standards. I walked over by the La Mamounia Hotel, which I had visited with Ali Karbush. I knew the La Mamounia would be too expensive, but I hoped I might find something else nearby. I glanced down a narrow street lined with palm trees and noticed a smaller hotel named Chems—"Sun Hotel"—that looked like it had been there for years. I discovered that it had a swimming pool, restaurant, bar, and clay tennis court. It was owned by an old family from Marrakech, and I dubbed it the mini Mamounia. I had a meeting with the son of the owner and told him of the group I would be bringing over in six months. We needed to have a large space available in the mornings for the classes, and I was wondering if we could use the garden. I mentioned that the group included older art students from America and that we would instruct them to be generous.

Now that I had secured the hotel, I needed to arrange the transportation for the group. I walked down Mohammed V Avenue on the way to Guilez, looking for car or van rentals. There weren't many since most people came on large tour buses, and the ones who did rent cars did so at the airport. I was lucky to find a rental business that had new VW buses for rent, which would be perfect for the artist groups. Introducing myself to the owner, I told him I would need three vans but not the drivers, and would pay for the insurance. He was new in the business and happy to have a new client, especially since I promised him there would be more business to come.

Linda and I had talked back in Santa Fe about how interesting it would be if we could bring in models so the artists could sketch them. We imagined hiring tattooed women with Berber capes and water men with their coin-filled bags and brass cups who sold water from goatskin bags. We talked about needing a location for the models to come for the art sessions and decided to ask Parisian about it. We wanted him to rent a large home with a spacious riad where the artists could sketch and paint. I spoke to Parisian the next night and told him of the artist groups and what it might mean for our business. He assured me he would find a perfect place in the ancient part of the city that would be close by and yet one that we could drive a van near to.

I went to the rug market that night, where there was a lot of action because the rugs had come from the Khemisset market. I recognized some of the weavings I had seen there, and some of the men also. I still had not received my rugs arriving on the CTM bus line. I had asked La Hassan to check on every bus for me and was beginning to get a little nervous. All I had was a small piece of paper with some numbers on it, and two days had already passed.

I left the rug market a little late and was walking out the small exit of the souk when a hand reached out and pulled me into a long narrow shop lit only by kerosene lanterns. As surprised as I was, I quickly saw that there were three men inside, two with saffron turbans, indicating they had been to Mecca, and one with a djellaba hood pulled down to his eyebrows. One of the men flashed me a smile of mostly gold teeth.

The man wearing the djellaba said, "I saw you at the Khemisset market a few days ago, and I am wondering if you had any *mushkiel*"—problems—"buying."

"No, I found some beautiful pieces at good prices, but I'm still waiting for my rugs to arrive on the CTM bus line."

All three men began speaking rapidly in Arabic, and then the djellaba man, who told me his name was Boujma, said, "We would like to help you. We saw that you did not come with a guide to Khemisset, and if you are willing to pay us the same price as you paid there, we will travel to the markets and bring the pieces that we think you will like back to Marrakech and show them to you here."

I told them I would show them my *goo*, the Berber word for *taste*, what I wanted them to buy and what I thought I could sell in America—tightly woven, authentic antique pieces from the villages. We scheduled a time the next evening for me to show them the pieces I was looking for—my goo.

I returned to the CTM and an excited La Hassan was waiting for me; my pieces had arrived on the bus from Casablanca. The duffle bags were a little beat up, but everything seemed intact. La Hassan carried the bags on his shoulder up to the second floor, where I eagerly unzipped them and spread them out in the courtyard. Now that I could see them again, they looked even more beautiful on the tile floor than when they were lying in the dirt. I hadn't made any mistakes.

After some time I was feeling sleepy but remembered Haj Midi's advice about always washing the rugs before bringing them into my room because of possible fleas, so I carefully refolded the rugs, placed them back into the duffle bags, and went into my room. I dreamed a vivid scene where men had saffron turbans and I was flying with them on a magic carpet.

I woke up early with the call to prayer, ready to clean the carpets so they would be dry by late afternoon. Later I was on the way to the afternoon market with the pieces I wanted to show Boujma and the saffron turban men. I walked through chicken alley, which then became beggar's alley, when I heard a man yell "Belek!"—"watch out!"—and the duffle bag was knocked off my shoulder and tumbled through the door of a boutique.

The owner of the store welcomed me in and said, "Good luck for me, I have been waiting for the foreigners to return." He told me he remembered the hippies from the early seventies and introduced himself as Klayna. He said he had had a tourist store in the medina for many decades. He was short, under five feet tall, with hair combed straight back, and I assumed it was difficult for him to find clothing his size since everything he wore was too large. He had a pleasant smile and a reassuring attitude, and I liked him immediately. As he guided me through the various rooms in the three-story building, it was obvious he had many items that would be perfect for our new store. One room had nothing but djellabas and caftans, so I told him about my upcoming artist group and how I needed to have caftans made for our customers. Klayna said he would love to help, and I added that I would also bring the group to his shop to buy souvenirs and perhaps another outfit for a Fantasia evening.

The Fantasia was something we had discussed with Doug as an evening of entertainment for the whole group. Held in a desert oasis outside of town, with enough tents for numerous tour groups, the Fantasia included food and music, ending with Berber men shooting their rifles into the sky while riding their galloping Arabian horses. A wide variety of musical groups came from different areas in the mountains, and the musicians played cymbals, castanets, fiddles, and three-string Gnowee guitars. Linda and I had been to the Fantasia earlier with Ben Ali, and we had seen the tour buses lining the parking lot. Everyone attending appeared to enjoy this Disney-like extravaganza, so we thought it would be a memorable last night for the tour, and Doug agreed.

I shook hands with Klayna and said I would be in touch. He motioned to one of his helpers to carry my duffle bag for me, and he followed me into the Berber market, which was close by. Outside the alley entrance he dropped my bag, knowing he shouldn't look like my guide. I picked up the bag, shook his hand with my folded dirhams as a tip, and headed into the market.

The three men I had met the night before were leaning against stacks of rugs when I entered, and all three said "Merhabban" at the same time. Perhaps doubting I would return, they were happy to see me. Boujma ordered tea, and the other men introduced themselves. The turbaned man with the gold teeth was Moulay, and the other man was Braheim.

The tea arrived, and we were all sitting on small wooden stools crammed against the rugs. I drank the one traditional glass of tea, then unzipped the duffle bag and pulled out the weavings. They examined and reexamined them and talked among themselves. Sometimes they would pull a rug out from one of the stacks to compare them. I sensed that what I had brought surprised them; most of the pieces they had were only what the tourists were buying. What was commonly in the market then were loosely woven pile rugs coming from the area of Chichoua, an area outside of Marrakech. These had large

graphic patterns and bold stripes on the ends and were traditionally either a bold deep red or an orange color. They were familiar with the antique weavings I was showing them but didn't think there was any market or value for them.

I took another leap of faith, thinking that Morocco had brought these men to me, and gave Boujma a deposit for him to go to the Khemisset market next week. Younger than Moulay and without the large family that Braheim had, Boujma was willing to travel on buses to the village markets. I knew that he would use my money and his credit to good effect and that I would have many things to look at next week, Enshalah.

I grabbed my rugs, zipped up my duffle bag, and walked farther into the rug souk. I took my time this evening and considered every shop carefully. I was taken by surprise when I saw a man observing the Berber market, sitting outside his store with a picture of President Carter. Intrigued, I entered into a large room with skylights, beautiful tile floors, and carpets lining the walls. One of his sons followed me in and introduced himself to me in perfect English, saying his name was Moulay Sherriff. I learned later that he was the oldest of four sons and had great appreciation for weavings, much like Abdulhey Midi.

His father was the leader of the rug market and helped to mediate disputes, even though he was of humble beginnings and had started off working as a plumber when he was a young man. I discovered later that Haj Midi and Haj Ben Sherriff had a lot in common, even though one was from the desert and the other was an Arab from the medina of Marrakech. Both men had good reputations and exquisite taste; each had great sources for weavings and were known to negotiate a good deal but always paid cash with no credit. For some unknown reason, both these older men took a liking to me, perhaps seeing something in me that they saw in themselves, which was a deep love of their country and its art. For many years Linda and I would be invited to celebrations of births, weddings, and religious festivals, and each man would pat the seat and have me sit down next to him. We would be the only foreigners, and it was a great honor and privilege.

I realized that Haj Ben Sherriff's store would be perfect for the large art group. I had thought earlier of taking the group to Haj Midi's farm, but the logistics would take too long to coordinate. So instead I discussed with Moulay the art group I was bringing in a few months. I suggested that he and I both present a talk on rugs in his store, followed by a large lunch in his father's home. I also told him that it was important not to raise the prices on the rugs, and that I would not be asking for any commission. I explained to him what I had observed already, which was that tourists were leaving Morocco with their money because they got so frustrated with the bargaining and felt they were being cheated. Moulay understood and agreed, and began to tell his father in Arabic about my artist tour idea. All the while Haj was looking at me, and I knew he instinctively understood. He nodded his thin face to me with a small smile.

I left the market feeling good about all I had accomplished that day. I wanted to call Linda and tell her the good news, and besides I missed hearing her voice. Finding a telephone and someone who would allow you to use it wasn't easy, but I told myself I would visit Parisian in the morning so I could use his telephone and call home.

Abdulhey happened to see me as I was about to leave the spice market, where he had gone to buy a few things for his mother. I related my visit to the Khemisset market, and he said, "If you liked the Khemisset market, you must come with me this January to the Imilchil market. My father's friend will lend us an old Land Rover, and we can buy a case of San Miguel beer and supplies here before we go. It is the first week of January, so come after Christmas and please buy a dozen American-made silver watches with large silver wrist straps. This will make the market so much more fun, and you will get a good education on how the Berbers do business." I responded that it sounded like fun and that I planned to join him.

I woke up the next morning, had my normal breakfast at the Café de France, and set out to meet Parisian. I wanted to check on the inventory of handbags he had made with Abslem and also to use his telephone to call Linda. I arrived at Parisian's shop as he was angrily moving a man with a vegetable cart from his doorway. The man set up there every morning, and this had become a ritual. When Parisian noticed me, he brightened up and ordered tea and some croissants from a young boy.

Parisian kept his phone under his desk, locked in a small, heavily carved wooden box with a padlock. He seldom used it, but liked knowing he owned one. I asked him if I could call Linda, and he said, "Of course, Enshalah," and left the shop for me to have some privacy. Linda was as excited as I was with all the arrangements I had made for Doug's group and told me her own news of additional handbag orders from Leon at the Dallas Market. Leon was wondering if we could expand the handbag line for the next gift market, and perhaps some home furnishings and other new styles, since Morocco was hot right now.

Being so far away from each other, missing each other, and sharing the same dreams, we kept talking and talking. Parisian came in, pointed to his watch, and I knew I needed to finish the conversation because long distance from Morocco was expensive. I headed back to the CTM and then the Iceberg for a shrimp omelet for lunch, missing Linda and feeling lonely, wishing she could be here.

On my way into the market that evening I stopped at Boujma 1's shop with the parrots. Now that I had met the younger Boujma with the rugs, I referred to them as Boujma 1 and Boujma 2. Earlier I had met a man who sold leather jackets to tourists and called himself Abdul 22, so Boujma 1 and 2 worked well for me. I bought Linda a nice woolen jacket with embroidery, which I knew she would look great in. I attended the rug auction but felt melancholy, so I left a little early.

Since I was heading back to the States in a few days, I decided I could use a haircut. A few beggars were outside the barbershop entrance when I arrived: one with no legs, another on crutches, and a woman with a young boy on her hip who appeared to be mentally impaired. In the shadows I saw another boy who was missing a foot and used a skateboard to get around the streets.

The barbershop had a small opening off the street and one bare lightbulb hanging from the ceiling. There must have been at least three old sinks, and I guessed that only one was really working. It was about eight o'clock at night, and few if any people wandered in to get their hair cut at this hour. Most of the men who went to a barber just had their heads or beards shaved. It was clear from the smell that many of his customers smoked cigarettes. I assumed this particular barbershop had been here about forty years because the yellowing paint on the walls, the chipped plaster, the pock-marked mirrors, and the old plastic combs all shouted out 1940.

Hanging on the yellow walls and propped up on the sinks was a collection of old eyeglasses and used sunglasses. This was a side business for the old barber—selling used bifocals to his Berber customers coming from the bus station—whose shop was near the square. Loud Islamic music was playing, mixed in with the Bee Gees coming from his neighbor's radio.

While I was there, people from the street continually peeked through the doorway, giving the barber suggestions. What started as a small trim was now a major operation. He kept moving my head up, then down, then pushed to one side, then the other. With no other customers, he spent a great deal of time cutting my hair. When he felt he was finished, he swept up all the hair on the floor so carefully that I thought he might be considering selling it to someone the next day.

I paid him with the only money I had left in my pocket, which was a fifty dirham note, not expecting any change. I suspected that haircuts cost perhaps fifty cents, so this was ten times that amount. He looked me right in the eyes, reached out for my right hand, and kissed my antique silver ring. As I exited his shop, he recited some sort of prayer. Back on the street I saw that the beggars had moved on, and as I passed all the dried fruit vendors selling figs and dates out of large burlap bags, I noticed I felt a lot cooler and thought I probably looked younger with my new haircut.

The next morning I went back to the fonduk to meet some of the other dealers whose shops had been closed when I had been there before. I found the fonduk as exciting as the Berber rug market. Semi-secret with a narrow-arched entryway, it was known only by local merchants, and most of the dealers were men, not from the mountains but from the desert oases in the south.

Bashir was there, so I sat with him first, drank tea, and looked through his latest acquisitions. He asked about Linda and picked out a pair of earrings that he said I should buy for her.

After I bought the earrings, I cruised the upstairs riad and entered a shop that had been closed when I was there before. The shop itself appeared not to have been cleaned in years, perhaps decades, and a broad assortment of items was thrown on top of each other randomly, so it was rather like a dirty treasure hunt to find anything. The owner, Haj Arby, wore a saffron turban and had a few front teeth missing. His family was from the far south, south of Dukala, in the Spanish Sahara. Haj Arby sold antique stone beads, ancient relics and silver charms from the desert, pottery, mats made from date palms and leather, camel bags, an assortment of camel-leather trappings, and other objects from the south of Morocco that I had never seen illustrated in *National Geographic* or displayed in museums.

A fascinating man, Haj Arby had two sons, one who was studying to become a lawyer, another interested in the artifact business and travel, and a daughter who was mentally impaired. Haj Arby had an open face and a kind smile, but he was totally illiterate, and it was challenging to negotiate with him. I would never forget one piece of pottery that I saw at his home during one of the first lunches he invited me to. Dating back to the 1840s or 1850s, it was exquisite with a bright aqua color and at least four inches thick and waist high. Haj offered it to me at a price that would have been more than $2,000 U.S. dollars to me—just hoping, or guessing, that he could catch a big fish. I gave little reaction and pretended not to notice. They lived with that piece of pottery for over a year in their front room, and every time I went to lunch there, I would try to negotiate the price. After that year I was doing so much business with him and his sons that he gifted the piece to me after lunch one day.

One of my most trusted employees for years was someone I named Abdul 1 since I had met so many Abduls. His nickname was Elvis because he wore his hair long, slicked back with hair goo, and was handsome. He had observed me walking every morning from the CTM Hotel, across the square and past the Café du Marrakech, which was where all the unofficial street guides would hang out, waiting for tourists who looked lost and had their pockets full of traveler's checks. All the other guides continually hounded me, day or night, but for some reason Abdul 1 never bothered me. Whether he was saving me for a bigger score, or had respect for me, I never knew.

I needed some guides to help me with the art groups, so one morning I stopped at his usual table at the café, where he was nursing a glass of water, and introduced myself. The cafés would allow a customer to sit with a glass of water an entire day without ordering anything else. It was just a Moroccan thing; most people had little if any money. Abdul pushed his sunglasses down low on his nose, looked me in the eye, and said, "I know who you are," in English.

I told him that I would be needing some assistance with some tour groups I was bringing to Marrakech, and that I would like him to help me. I also mentioned I would need a few other guides, so maybe he could ask some of his friends. Enshalah. He said, "You can count on me, I will help you."

My last two days in Morocco I had a bad bout of food poisoning. Even though I tried to be careful, and stuck with my shrimp omelets, I sometimes got it. There was always a parasite lurking nearby. This time my feet ached as well, so between the vomiting and diarrhea it was extremely painful to walk. Thankfully I had already picked up all my purchases and packed my duffle bags for the return trip. Brecka came to me late in the afternoon with a small lighted stick and mumbled some prayers, and the next day I did feel better and was able to travel to Casablanca to catch the plane. I slumped into my 56K seat, drank only one Schlitz Malt Liquor, and tried to sleep all the way to

New York.

By the time the plane landed I felt a little bit better and used my standard trick of going through U.S. customs by finding a line with an older male customs official who I assumed was ready to retire. I had asked Parisian to give me some of his blank invoices and had written up my own just in case I was asked to show any. I wrote some numbers and what I thought looked like Arabic, and used Parisian's ink stamps all over them to make them look official, knowing that if someone could read Arabic, he or she would not be a customs agent. Linda picked me up at the Albuquerque airport, and I was delighted to be reunited with her and back in the States.

Chapter Eight

Bicycles and Pencils

◇◇◇◇◇◇◇◇◇◇◇◇◇◇◇◇◇◇◇◇◇◇◇◇◇◇◇◇◇◇◇◇◇◇◇◇◇◇

THE STORE had been doing well, and Linda was excited to see me and what I had brought back. I opened my carry-on bag and spread out all the new treasures. I described meeting Haj Arby and showed her the collection of small jewelry pieces. She was fascinated by all the trinkets and charms and laughed as I told her how my bargaining with Haj Arby had taken well over an hour. All the items looked like they had been used or worn for centuries, so we couldn't wait to clean, polish, and wear them. I also said Parisian was shipping the handbags in the post, so we should have them in a few weeks. We had a lot of new inventory for the store, including the fabulous new rugs from Khemisset.

Leon's statement about the popularity of Moroccan items was evident at our next gift show in Dallas, with the demand rising into a huge wave that we were now skillfully surfing. We continued to pack and ship boxes every day for the handbag orders, and got to know our UPS driver well.

The questionnaires we had sent to Doug's art group had all come back with their sizes and favorite colors. We ended up with eighteen women and two men, plus Doug.

We went to the Santa Fe flea market looking for used clothing for the poor and some new baseball caps for our friends in the market. We also found some T-shirts for Jazz Man that had been samples for silk screening and were covered with logos in English, and we bought all the ones the seller had. They were labeled Fruit of the Loom and Made in America, so we knew Jazz Man would like them.

When the tour was set to start in two weeks, Linda and I left for Morocco ahead of time, bringing Igloo ice chests as our luggage, plus two disassembled mountain bikes packed in what became misshapen duffle bags. Linda and I had discovered that bikes were the best way to get around Marrakech, and we wanted to have our own there.

Flying a new route from Madrid to the Menara airport in Marrakech, we breezed through customs because Parisian had already tipped the douane agents, some of whom were friends of his from the mosque. He met us outside the airport and had a Mercedes taxi waiting to take us to our newly rented house in Bab Dukala. Out of nowhere a lieutenant, the new head of customs, tapped me on the shoulder and motioned me to follow him back to his office. I told Linda to stay with the taxi; I would handle this. I rehired the porters to bring the baggage and headed back to the airport, following the official through a door that read "Customs Officials, No Admittance."

Parisian followed along with the driver of the taxi but was stopped short of the large metal door with a picture of the king on it. The douane head led me to a smaller room, leaving Parisian and the taxi driver outside in the heat, and told me to sit, not stand. The room smelled like mint tea, and several low-level customs agents lined the walls.

I soon understood that no one was interested in the two neatly packed Igloo ice chests, just the two misshapen duffle bags. The head official unzipped one duffle bag and pulled out the handle bars to one of the bikes. He then pulled out the bicycle seats and finally the frame. He sat down behind an old, large metal desk in front of another picture of the king. In one swift movement he produced a large ledger and searched for an empty page. "Passport, please," he said. I handed over my passport and watched as he became confused at all the extra visa stamps. I glanced over to the walls and saw the other agents grinning because most of them recognized me and had been tipped by me before.

The lieutenant said that he would record the bikes in his ledger and I could have the bikes back if I agreed to take them back to the States when I leave, or, if I wanted to keep them here, that I would need to pay a tax. He asked me how much they cost, and I replied that I had bought them used for 500 dirhams each (about fifty dollars) at a flea market like the one in Bab el Khemis.

"Impossible" he said, and I told him I was a good bargainer. He stood up, straightened his tie, and said the tax would be 4,000 dirhams, about $400, for both. I replied that I needed them for my business so I could ride around the medina and keep the beggars and guides from following me. We went around and around—he, telling me I needed to pay for both, and I, explaining I was a friend of Morocco and doing much business in his country and helping the people.

Finally, he became exasperated and said, "Fine, just take the bikes." I said, "No, I would love to pay the tax, but for only one of the bikes. Perhaps you could just forget the other one?" With that he shook my hand as I handed him the dirhams for the tax, and wrote only one bike down in the ledger on his desk and then closed it.

I realized I had worn him down and could have accepted his offer to bring both bikes in tax-free, but by offering to pay some of the tax, I had allowed him to save face in front of the other agents.

As I was walking out the door with all my bags repacked, I asked him if there was anything he would like from the States on my next trip. "Just a few new silk neckties," he replied. We were friends for years after that exchange. Parisian laughed when I told him about paying the tax for only one of the bikes.

The next morning we went to the Chems Hotel and confirmed that all the rooms were reserved and that the garden area would be available every morning for classes. Then we were off to see Klayna to give him the list of all the sizes and colors of the clothing we needed tailored. He assured us they would be done in time. Next we set out to see Moulay Sherriff and arrange the date for the talk in his rug gallery and the luncheon at his father's home. The last thing to confirm was the vans from the rental car company, so we rode our new bikes down Mohammed V and were assured that the three vans would be available for our ten-day tour.

Later Linda and I walked over to meet with Abdul 1 at his favorite café on the square. We found him at his usual table, and he greeted me with a strong handshake and Linda with a kiss on both cheeks.

I ordered some kawa halib and croissants for each of us and described to him what we had planned for the group. We explained that the art instruction would occupy the mornings, and the afternoons would be devoted to excursions and shopping. We also included a few trips for the group, one to the Ourika Valley Market, and the other an overnight trip to Essaouira. Abdul mentioned there was a camel market we should visit on our way back from Essaouira.

I asked him if he had found any friends who could also help us with the group, and he answered, "Of course, my brother," with a huge smile. Abdul confessed that the only thing a little odd was that they all had the same name, Abdul. I had already learned that in Morocco the first son was named Mohammed, and Abdul was a common second or third son's name, with the traditional meaning of "servant of God," so it wasn't surprising that all the young men had the same name. I told Abdul 1 we would just call them Abdul 1 through 4.

We arranged a time later that day for me to meet the other Abduls alone without Linda. During the meeting I soon discovered they all had not one but three other facts in common: they were all unofficial guides in the markets, they all lived in the Kasbah, and lastly, they all had no fathers around and served as the breadwinners for their family (and apparently each of their oldest brothers was away, unable to work, or simply unindustrious).

For the tour group I would dress all the Abduls in the same khaki outfits that the medina police wore, which made for lots of fun since there was no love lost between the police and the Abduls. The medina police would always shake down these unofficial guides for money. One afternoon before the tour arrived, Abdul 1 and I were walking across the square, both wearing sunglasses, when a policeman approached us for the shakedown. He spoke to Abdul 1 in Arabic as I just stood there, and when he looked over at me, I pulled my sunglasses down on my nose so he could see my blue eyes. The policeman then pushed my glasses back up over my eyes, and I asked, "*Ash be tee?*"—"what do you want?" He replied in perfect English, "In Morocco you never ask the police what they want," and walked away.

Once the tour had begun I would have the Abduls come to my

rented house every evening after the last prayers to pay them for the day and to instruct them on what we planned to do tomorrow. After that we would have one tequila shot from Mexico, which they re-named "To Kill You."

The next week went by quickly. Brecka found models for the artists, and we made all the arrangements for the overnight trip to Essaouira. We would also stay at a Chems Hotel there, which was owned by the La Mamounia hotel chain. Linda and I stayed up at night in Bab Dukala planning each day's events and hoping we had not forgotten anything that needed to be arranged.

Finally the day arrived and the tour group landed in Marrakech. Parisian had paid out several "tips," so our group was able to get through customs quickly. We welcomed them and led them to the horse-drawn carriages I had hired so they could enter the city the same way I had on my first trip, which had made such an impression on me. Abdul 1 drove one of the vans with all the luggage.

Once everyone was settled at the Chems, I gathered the group

for a short talk. I handed out the clothes from Klay-na and then asked everyone to hold out their hands, which I filled with some small coins. I told them the coins were for the beggars and said I hoped they had brought over the hard candy and used clothing like we had suggested. I also asked them to please not buy anything their first day because it could be so confusing, and explained that Morocco was a country of no refunds or returns. Then I looked at the eighteen women, smiled, and said, "Please do not indulge your Omar Sharif fantasies here." They all laughed, and we ended the first evening.

The art classes held in the morning were engaging. Doug was an excellent teacher, and the garden cool and comfortable. The three vans worked out perfectly. I drove one, Linda another, and Abdul 1 the third. Packed with activities, every day seemed to be going well. For the drive to the market in the Ourika Valley in the mountains east of Marrakech, we had instructed everyone to be at the vans by six a.m. because the market opened at daybreak. Since I had been to Khemisset, I knew what to expect, but for the rest of the group, seeing the masses of people walking or riding donkeys or horse-drawn wagons to the markets in the early light was fascinating. Once there I told everyone we would meet back at the vans in four hours, and not to be late.

The artists took their easels and stools and found a place they wished to sketch. Linda and I were walking around the market when I felt a tap on my shoulder. I turned around to see a man who appeared to be the *kaid*, the leader of Ourika. He gestured for me to follow him to a small cement building with the Moroccan flag displayed. I told Linda to wait for me outside, and I entered the room.

He directed me to sit and then asked in English, "Who are you? Where are you from? And who are these people you have brought here to the market?"

"I am T.R. Lawrence. I am an American and I do business in Marrakech. They are all university art students."

He stared at me doubtfully. "They seem too old to be students."

"In America, people go back to the university at older ages."

He proceeded to ask me more questions, and I explained they only wish to sketch and paint. That appeared to calm him down, especially when I also shook his hand with my folded-up square of dirhams, and then he told me I could leave. On my way out the door he said, "No photographs, only sketches, and you are always welcome to come back, Enshalah."

About an hour later Linda and I heard a lot of screaming and commotion by the stream that runs through the market. We hurried over and saw a large group of people yelling and chasing a young boy who was running for his life. The boy was caught and brought back to the area where a member of the tour had set up an art easel.

Abdul 1 was there and told me the young boy had stolen a pencil from the artist, and the people had been chasing the boy to stone him—the punishment for stealing. Abdul said the punishment was severe because all the people were poor, and they could not allow anyone to be a thief. The boy appeared to be about eight years old and was sobbing.

We asked Abdul to explain to the villagers that if the young boy would give the pencil back to the artist and apologize, that would be enough for us. We also asked him to say how difficult it was for this young boy to see all these strange artists with their many pencils, and that the temptation was too great for someone so young. The people all grudgingly agreed, and the young boy returned the pencil to the artist. Thankfully, the four hours were just about up, so we all headed to the vans and back to Marrakech.

The artists who had brought over the used clothes ended up being "repaid" with experiences they probably hadn't anticipated. We suggested they give them to whoever they wished, and most of them picked a favorite waiter or maid. They were rewarded with ice-cold glasses of orange juice as they floated in the pool, and many were even invited to the person's home for a lunch or mint tea. We took all the guests shopping at my merchant friends' shops in the souks, and later when I walked through the alleys, the owners tried to shove money into my pockets—my commission—which I always refused and told them to keep it for their children. My reputation only got better, and soon everyone wanted to help me.

The luncheon at the Villa of Bazar du Sud, Moulay Sherriff's father's home, was a huge success. The rugs were thrown around the tile fountain, and Moulay and I spoke about the tribes and how to spot a good rug from the tourist junk. Moulay had outdone himself, even hiring some musicians to play while the group ate the many courses he had provided. Young servant girls hustled to and from the kitchen in the back of the home with well-laden brass trays, and the food was extraordinary. In the end our group had purchased many antique saffron carpets from the High Atlas, and Moulay, who had convinced his father to open his home to a group of foreigners, was extremely pleased.

Essaouira was an excellent side trip the next day. On the way there everyone enjoyed seeing the goats climbing and walking on the limbs of the argan trees while they were searching for the tasty nuts. The road was blacktop but only about one and a half lanes wide, so passing a bus in the Volkswagen vans was difficult. As we entered Essaouira we were stopped by a spiked chain that was drawn across the highway by the Royal Moroccan Gendarmerie. The royal policemen were big and intimidating, dressed in knee-high boots, khaki outfits, and Ray-Ban sunglasses with mirrorlike lenses. They asked for everyone's passport and examined them behind one of the vans. I gave them a few minutes before I got out and joined the police. I was asked the standard questions: "Who are you, what are you doing, and who is this group?" I spotted who I thought must be the commandant and introduced myself to him. With my folded dirhams in my palm, I gave him a hard, firm handshake, and he said, "Welcome to Essaouira."

It was an ideal location for the artists to sketch and paint, given the exceptional variety of subject matter: the fortress with the cannons, the narrow streets, the women all wrapped in white blankets, and the shipbuilding. Linda and I had known the group would enjoy this respite from the souk and the hustle of Marrakech. After two active days in the sea air, including meals of large sardines and black lobsters at Chez Sam, everyone was exhausted and slept all the way back to Marrakech.

The next day the group came to the rented house in Bab Dukala. The artists had been told we would have models dressed in traditional clothing for them to sketch in the garden. Brecka arrived with some of her Berber neighbors, many with tribal tattoos and exotic clothing. She convinced them that no photographs would be taken, so they didn't have to worry or be frightened about a camera stealing their soul. She also told them they would be paid and given a sketch of themselves. It was highly rewarding for both the artists and the models, and we talked about it all the way back to the Chems Hotel.

At the next morning's class Doug critiqued the sketches of the models, and everyone was enthusiastic about their accomplishments. That evening we drove everyone to the Fantasia for our farewell party. Twelve tour buses were parked outside the large black-and-white tents, and for each group of tourists Berber women would join hands, forming an inner circle, and dance before the guests. It reminded me of the dancers at the Kodak Hula Show in Honolulu, where I grew up. There were a multitude of performers, including a young woman who balanced a brass tray on her head filled with lit candles as she slithered from the floor to a standing position.

Following a meal replete with red wine and cold couscous with lemon chicken, members of our group danced with a bunch of Italian dentists. The dentists had mistakenly purchased women's caftans and djellabas to wear for the Fantasia, so it looked like women dancing with women as the beat vibrated off the desert sand dunes outside of town.

When the ten days were over, with everyone in the group having had a wonderful experience, Doug asked us if we would do it again. After conducting two more art group retreats with Doug, and one with a theater group out of Houston, Linda and I decided to hang up our hats as tour operators. The police in Marrakech were beginning to harass me every time I showed up with a group, and it was taking a lot of time and energy from our Nomads business, so we left the tour business to others.

Trading Watches and Escaping Weirdos

◇◇◇◇◇◇◇◇◇◇◇◇◇◇◇◇◇◇◇◇◇◇◇◇◇◇◇◇◇◇◇◇◇◇

Two months later, after spending some time in the States, I was back on the plane flying to Marrakech to visit the Imilchil market with Abdulhey. I brought with me my bags of used clothes for the poor and warm clothes for me to wear in the mountains. I had bought twelve watches at the flea market, taken them out of their boxes, and put them into socks that I then shoved into my tennis shoes, which I packed in my carry-on bag.

I arrived in Marrakech a few days after Christmas, so it allowed Abdulhey and me time to prepare for the market. He told me his father had rented one of the few buildings there for us to sleep in and conduct our business, because the other alternative was to spend the night in tents like the rest of the travelers. The vintage Land Rover came with extra fuel cans and looked to serve us well. We set off early on December 29, hoping to beat the buyers from Fez, who Abdulhey said we would meet but wouldn't like. Everyone always said that they were different, they never took no for an answer, and they bargained you down until there wasn't any profit left. We traveled the same road out of Marrakech that I took for the Khemisset market, but fifty miles outside of town we turned right toward the High Atlas Mountains.

Abdulhey was a good driver and took his time negotiating the switchback gravel roads. This was a barren part of Morocco, and I saw few villages in the distance and some walking trails leading from the road, seeming to go nowhere. I observed that all the people who were approaching us in the other lane put their hands on the windshield, and I asked Abdulhey about it. He explained that they thought it would prevent them from getting a cracked windshield.

Right before we arrived, Abdulhey asked me if I had brought the watches with me. "Of course, I want the education in bargaining you promised me."

We reached the top of the mountain and saw a small valley below with little vegetation and a stream running through it. There were a few cement buildings, one with a Moroccan flag flying out front. People were already assembling their tents for sleeping, and other tents would serve as restaurants.

Since he had been there before, Abdulhey drove right to the building. Two cots were set up next to the walls, with some dirty sheepskins on them. It was a five-hour trip, and both of us were tired, so I made sandwiches with the dried beef and bread I had brought along and shared them with Abdulhey. We drank two beers, smoked some of his hashish, and I fell asleep while he was still questioning me about my life in America.

No call to prayer here, just the steady pounding of horse hooves and squeaking of wagons. By daybreak the valley looked completely different. Hundreds of people had come during the night and were busy setting up tents.

We found someone to make us tea, ate some stale bread from the night before, and got ready to meet and greet Haj Midi's friends who were looking for Abdulhey. As a young boy he always came to the market with his father, so many men came up to greet him. He asked me to put on my old blue cape with the holes in it, a stocking cap, and my sunglasses so I didn't look so out of place. He also wanted both of us to wear one of the watches. He told me to be patient, keep my money hidden, and only pay people in private.

I could already feel people admiring the watches, and it didn't take long for one of them to want to trade. I instantly recognized this man as someone I had met at the CTM Hotel. He had knocked on my door to ask me if I had any American jewelry I would like to trade or sell. I was curious, so I followed him to his small room by the stairs, where he opened two old leather suitcases filled with necklaces of amber, coral, and amazonite. I was wearing a silver and turquoise belt buckle that I offered to trade for one of the necklaces. The lines on his face and his deep suntan told a story of a man who spent his life traveling the mountains by foot, horseback, or bus, trading with the Berber tribes. Now I was with him again in Imilchil, and he could not keep his eyes off my watch, so I offered it to him to inspect. Luckily I had bought all self-winding watches, because the first thing he did was to shake it and look at the back plate to see where it was made.

The Berber men all wanted silver watches with silver wrist bands, not leather straps, since this had become a status symbol among them. Abdulhey told him the market had not yet begun and to come back tomorrow morning to see if we wanted to do any business.

We had an excellent location before the entrance to the fair, and many people got to see us wearing the watches. Some were interested in me and what I was doing there, but most of them were too shy to stop and ask Abdulhey. The traders who knew Haj Midi asked us if they could leave their carpets and capes with us for safe keeping. That gave us a chance to look at them before the others. Some of the pieces looked like the pictures I had seen in *National Geographic*, while others resembled old American Indian weavings from the Southwest. Many were antique pieces, tightly woven and in mixed condition I had found a few men in Marrakech recently who could repair and reweave pieces that were damaged, so these pieces interested me because they would be sold cheaper.

The market was turning out to be much more than I had expected. There were few cars or trucks here, so our Land Rover stood out among the animals in the parking lot. By late afternoon enough merchants were interested in the watches that I could have traded with all of them. No one asked for my price, just what I wanted in trade. It was hard for me to understand that in the 1980s these people had no hard currency and still lived using a bartering system, which to me was like living in a Biblical era.

That evening Abdulhey and I sat on the weavings we were intending to buy, in our warm cement building, and watched the people huddling around campfires. We both praised Allah for how lucky our lives were.

The morning brought a rush of men all wanting to trade for the watches. Abdulhey and I let them bargain among themselves and settle on the amount they thought they were worth. I traded for some necklaces from the man I had met at the CTM Hotel. Another watch went to a local kaid from a neighboring village who traded me two beautiful rugs that had been in his family for years. He quickly rolled up his sleeves and put the watch on his wrist so everyone could see it. I kept the one on my wrist till the last minute and traded it to a tribal chieftain for a long wool-and-silk tent wall. I had now successfully traded for more than ten carpets and capes, some necklaces, and a few antique silver daggers. With the money I had brought, I purchased another fifteen weavings.

Abdulhey was still wearing his watch and told me he would trade it for something from his collection. I told him to keep it as a memento for him to remember our trip to Imilchil together.

We left the market early the next morning before the Berber Bridal Fair began, when everyone's attention turned from trading to arranging marriages. I had tried to get some information about the fair but found only one article written many years ago in *National Geographic*. The article didn't provide much information, but the photographs of the people all wearing their black-and-white-striped capes did arouse my interest. On the way back to Marrakech, Abdulhey explained the ceremonies and traditions of the one-hundred-year-old bridal fair. I found it interesting that the women would wear the capes on their heads in different shapes, either rounded or peaked, showing everyone if the woman had been married before or was a virgin. If she had been married before, the marriage could take place immediately. If she was a virgin, the marriage would be delayed until the next year, after all the dowry arrangements had been made. The wedding vow in Berber was simply "I give you my liver." The wedding contracts were written in either Berber or Arabic on a small wooden stick that would then have a red-ink government seal to show its legality. I would buy many of these contract sticks whenever I found them in the market in years to come—to sell them as the perfect wedding or anniversary gift back at Nomads. What Abdulhey told me was fascinating, but I was more fascinated by my acquisitions in the back of the Land Rover.

Abdulhey then questioned me about the Indian jewelry from Santa Fe. Haj Midi had expressed an interest in the silver and turquoise jewelry of the Native Americans early on, beginning from the very first day I met them. Once I told them about moving to Santa Fe, they asked if I would be willing to buy Indian jewelry and bring it to Morocco, where we could trade for the antique Berber jewelry in Haj Midi's overflowing trunks.

"Enshalah," I said.

Back in Santa Fe, Linda and I began scoping out the Santa Fe flea market, Trader Jacks, every weekend for authentic Indian jewelry. The legendary Trader Jacks was located north of town near the Santa Fe Opera. It had been happening for years before we arrived in Santa Fe and continued for another ten or more afterward—a wild conglomeration of old hippies, new and old artists, misfits, travelers, and people just cleaning out their garages. Every weekend provided a new discovery. We found beautiful pawn bracelets, rings, and earrings. Training our eye, within a few weeks we had acquired an excellent collection to bring to Haj Midi and Abdulhey.

About six weeks later I was back in Morocco, having carried all my Indian jewelry in either my socks, pant pockets, or mixed up with other personal items in the same carry-on bag. I took another carriage ride to the CTM Hotel, where Haj Midi, Abdulhey, and their driver, Weasel, were patiently waiting for me to arrive. They had parked in the underground parking garage beneath the hotel, where there were few eyes to observe. Weasel was on the lookout for me, and when he saw me get out of the carriage, he quickly ushered me to Haj Midi who was waiting in the car. Following the usual round of handshakes and cheek kisses, I slowly unzipped the canvas bags and brought out the jewelry. I smiled as their eyes lit up; they had never seen American Indian jewelry before, only in photographs.

Haj and Abdulhey began speaking rapidly in Arabic and clutched some of the pieces to their chest, not wanting to let go. "*Tamum, gulia tamum*"—"How much? Tell me how much," they said. I responded that we needed a scale, a balance, to weigh the silver and determine the price, so we agreed to meet the next day at Haj Midi's shop.

I packed up my bags, found La Hassan to carry them, and walked wearily up the chipped stairs to my corner room. After a few short hours the morning call to prayer reached me wide awake, so I went up to the rooftop to say hello to Brecka.

Brecka was happy to see me and told me she had received the other postcard. I helped her hang the heavy, wet sheets, then went downstairs and next door for my favorite coffee with milk before winding my way to the rug souk. Abdulhey and Haj were already

waiting for me and immediately ordered a young boy to bring us kawa halib to drink. While we were waiting, I noticed the scale near-by, so I motioned to Abdulhey that we should get started. I brought out the jewelry and once again observed the gleam in their eyes as they started looking at what I had brought from Trader Jacks.

Abdulhey and Haj gathered a large pile of what they wanted, and once the pieces were weighed it was easy to tell them the price without any bargaining. They said they were willing to help me sell the rest of the jewelry in Agadir, a major city on the coast in mid-southern Morocco. I was aware of it because of Anchor Point, the popular surfing destination. It is near the foot of the Atlas Mountains where the Sous River flows into the ocean, creating a fabulous river surf break. Wearing full-on wet suits because the Atlantic waters are freezing, the surfers jump off the rocks to enter the water, holding their boards tightly.

We agreed to leave for Agadir after the first prayers of the morning, and they would pick me up in Haj's car, with Weasel driving. The distance from Marrakech was about ninety miles, which would be about a one-and-half-hour car ride in the States, yet here would take nearly four hours.

As soon as we left Marrakech, we encountered heavy fog even though we were still hours away from Agadir and fog rarely crept this far inland. The landscape visible from the road was completely barren, with the Anti-Atlas Mountain range totally obscured on our left. We passed few gas stations and roadside cafes as we drove on. I occasionally saw a few people with their backs to the highway, supposedly waiting for a bus, but I wondered where they came from. There weren't any visible houses or buildings on the side of the road, nor even crossroads or paths that I could detect.

I glanced over at Haj, who was eating a sandwich that he had hidden in the hood of his djellaba, and at Abdulhey who was fast asleep, and then at Weasel, who kept his eyes on the road. He was not a relative, so he knew he was expendable and did whatever it took to keep his job.

Soon after we arrived, the fog lifted, and we strolled along the beach. We stood out—a strange group all dressed in our full-length djellabas while the rest of the people on the beach were in shorts or swimsuits, and some sunbathed topless. These topless women created a major distraction for the vendors and the camel jockeys.

The owners of the few stores we visited knew Haj and Abdulhey and welcomed the new merchandise. Abdulhey handled the negotiations for me, and later when I had a pocketful of dirhams, I noticed the merchants kissing the American Indian bracelets as they put them into their showcases.

On the drive back to Marrakech, Abdulhey said that Haj asked him to tell me not to mention to anyone about selling the Indian jewelry. Abdulhey pointed out that if people see you making money, then all your distant relatives, or the government, suddenly want to be your new business associate.

I spent another ten days buying from all my friends, and then it was time to leave. After my final day of purchasing I walked back to the CTM Hotel and found the square mostly empty since it was now late afternoon and the hottest part of the day. At the hotel I saw La Hassan and Omar nodding to each other. They knew I would be leaving later that day and, as before, let me have the room for a few more hours after the designated checkout time. Taxis were always lined up outside the hotel, so it was easy to hire one. I tossed the duffle bags filled with handbags and rugs into the trunk of one of the taxis, said the perfunctory "Peacemela"—"God protect me"—and we headed out through the crowds to the train station.

Even though I was early, the station was already overcrowded with people, mostly men in the military. I was told that the military got to travel for free on the trains, and these soldiers were coming from fighting against the Polisario in the Sahara Desert. The train was running late, which wasn't anything new, and while I waited I bought a better ticket for a business compartment.

When the train finally showed up in the late afternoon, it was billowing black smoke and resembled a scene out of the American Civil War. There were lots of handshakes and cheek-kissing and tears. Then everyone ran for the train even though it was still moving. Amid lots of whistle-blowing I found my compartment, and to my surprise I was the only one ticketed for it. As I gazed out the window while there was still light, I could see small villages with one-story buildings in the distance, and occasionally people dressed in brown djellabas leading camels or donkeys beside the railroad tracks.

After two hours the train suddenly stopped, but only for a few minutes. What happened next would be etched forever in my mind. I looked out my compartment door and saw the train conductor escorting a large, heavily bearded man wearing numerous fur-skin coats and carrying a drum strapped to his back. They both walked down the aisle past me, but a few minutes later they returned, and the conductor opened the door, shoved the bearded man into my compartment, and closed the door.

This man stood directly in front of me, studied me up and down, from my long hair to the henna-dyed finger nails that Brecka had given me, and smiled widely. He then sat down in front of me on a bench with our knees almost touching. He smiled at me again and then made a movement with his fingers going back and forth through a hole he had created using the thumb and forefinger of his left hand. He did this for a minute and then quickly reached over and grabbed a hunk of my hair and banged his head into mine. He caught me totally by surprise, and before I could react he made the finger movements again. I understood then that he wanted to screw me, so I impulsively grabbed the back of his head and smashed my head into his.

This changed the situation immediately. He smiled at me again and then reached into his pocket and produced an unfiltered cigarette that he pushed into my mouth. At that very moment the train conductor and a few of his friends entered the compartment and were all laughing loudly as they ushered the bearded man and his drum out. A few minutes later the conductor returned to tell me that the bearded passenger with the fur coat and drum had recently been released from prison where he had served a ten-year sentence for manslaughter. He then told me he pushed him into my compartment as a joke and hoped it didn't offend me.

Chapter Ten

Learning a Few New Lessons

◇◇◇◇◇◇◇◇◇◇◇◇◇◇◇◇◇◇◇◇◇◇◇◇◇

L IFE HUMMED ALONG as we kept busy at Nomads and continued to expand our line of products, working six days a week and attending the twice-yearly Dallas gift shows with Leon. I returned to Morocco about every eight weeks. Linda usually came with me about every third trip, so we both were busy, having fun, and living the dream.

I always went to see what Boujma 2 had found for me when I first arrived and was never disappointed. My first afternoon back I purchased some carpets from him, loaded up the mashu, and took them to the Bab Dukala warehouse. That night while looking at them all again, I was excited about most of them, but there were a few mixed in that I had not selected. They were not my taste, and they didn't belong in Nomads. I knew I could have kept them; Boujma wouldn't have known since I did all the paperwork and added the figures. But I determined to return the three pieces to him.

As I was putting them on the back of my bicycle the next morning to head back into the souk, Parisian happened to come by. He asked me what I was doing with the carpets, and I explained that Boujma had given them to me by mistake, that I had not paid for them. Parisian then said, "Lawrence, you should just keep them. Those people are making so much money off you, you should just take them." I straddled my bicycle with the heavy load behind me and said, "But it's not my way," and out the door into the traffic I cycled. From that gesture I earned Boujma's trust, and he began to treat me even more like a family member.

One afternoon I was sitting in the rug market with Boujma. I was waiting for the auction to begin, and in his small shop I recognized some of the men I had seen at the auction every week. These were not local merchants but men who traveled on the buses to the remote areas and village markets looking for the antique textiles. I was told they sometimes even knock on people's doors to ask if there were any old weavings there.

I decided it was about time to pay for tea, so I handed a young boy a hundred dirham note, about the equivalent of ten dollars, and asked him to bring me tea and get me change. The mint tea cost only a few dirhams. After about forty-five minutes the boy had delivered the tea, but he still hadn't yet gotten the change for me. Eventually my money arrived, but it took over an hour.

In the meantime I asked Boujma and his friends to show me their wallets. Reluctantly, they all reached into their djellabas and each pulled out at least two and sometimes three wallets—I guess I was that persuasive. I asked why they had that many, and they said one of the wallets was for brand-new money, the second for the money they used most often, and the third only for the very old money—torn, soiled, and crumpled so badly the banks would not accept them— that they gave to the beggars.

Only one man of the four had any money at all, a rug guy from Casablanca. The others, including my friend Boujma, had only small slips of white paper with Arabic numbers on them. These were the IOUs they all carried, or what they called "papers of Enshalah," either with names and numbers of those who owed them money, or those they owed money to. This credit system was how the whole souk operated.

I resolved to help my new friend Boujma 2 get a bank account. This way he would be able to accept my checks—papers of Enshalah but with more of a guarantee—and get the money within thirty days. I had met the bank representative at Banc du Maroc many times while I was exchanging money. His name was Claude, a French Moroccan, and he hoped to be branch president of the bank one day at the Djemma el Fna. On my first visit he had ushered me into his office and questioned me about the money I was exchanging and what I was going to use it for. Claude loved the idea of my sending the antiques from Morocco to the States; he had passion for them himself.

It took hours to exchange money. Not only did the bank tellers do the same things as the money changers, which was to make sure there wasn't any ink on the bills or any tears, but they also checked every single serial number. They had been told that the Russians had printed counterfeit hundred-dollar bills, so they weren't taking any chances.

The morning after the revelation that no one had any money in their pockets, I was at the bank to meet with Claude. He asked if I needed any assistance. "Yes, please," I responded. "I promise to exchange all the money I bring to Morocco here at your bank, but I would like to bring you a new customer who doesn't trust the bank, and I need you to help him." I told Claude that I had convinced my friend Boujma to come and open an account, but that he was from the mountains and nervous about doing so. I also asked Claude to bring Boujma into his private office every time he saw him come in so he could avoid what were always long lines at the bank. Claude agreed, we shook hands, and Boujma 2 opened his first bank account. Claude honored his promise that Boujma never had to stand in line, which made my friend feel very important.

Later, when word got out that my checks were always good, everyone wanted to do business with me. It speeded up our transactions and made it easier for me since I didn't have to carry in so much cash or traveler's checks from America.

Boujma was a devout man and a great businessman. He had a beautiful Berber wife, three sons, and two daughters. Every trip, whether Linda was with me or not, I would be invited to a wonderful long lunch with many other family members in attendance. I would bring over new clothes for his children so they would be well dressed for school. His two older boys became great little helpers to me, and I spoke with Boujma about his boys learning English at the American Institute in Marrakech. Boujma was modern in his thinking, so when I offered to pay for the boys' schooling, he agreed. When the boys each turned about twelve years old, I wanted to buy them a bicycle. Again Boujma agreed, and I took them with me and told them to pick the bicycle of their dreams. They both chose a white one, probably because Marrakech was so dirty. I asked Boujma later if he felt I had Westernized his two sons too much, and he replied that whenever I leave, they go back to being good Muslim boys.

One day when I was alone I was invited to lunch at Boujma's house with both Boujma and his partner Braheim. While we were waiting for the couscous, Boujma asked me a few questions I knew he had been wondering about. Boujma brought up the subject of children. He wondered why I didn't have any. Then he asked if maybe I wasn't able to have any, or if I was just too shy to ask Linda. He then asked if perhaps Linda was unable to have children. I answered no to all the questions and just said I didn't like them.

Boujma couldn't understand that, so I finally said if he wanted me to have one, why doesn't he just give me the little boy sitting in the corner? I said I would take him to the States and eventually send him to the university. Boujma took me seriously and replied that they had already named the little boy and loved him, so that would not be possible. But then Boujma went into the kitchen and brought in a woman who was pregnant and said I could have this one when it was born because they didn't know it yet. Or he could bring me another woman that I could have a family with. It took me quite a while that day to convince Boujma and Braheim that Linda and I did not want any children, but I thanked him for his kind offers.

On my next trip to Morocco, Linda accompanied me. We wanted to travel to some other villages and explore the southern part of Morocco, so when all our other business was completed in Marrakech, we rented a Toyota version of a Land Rover from the same agency where we got the VW vans years earlier. We picked up a few supplies as we left town on the road to Agadir. As we passed Agadir and headed south, the road was reduced to one and a half lanes and seemed to crumble, with lots of gravel, and was traveled mainly by taxis and just a few trucks driving between the villages.

Our first stop was Tiznit, a city renowned for producing the enameled silver Berber jewelry we loved. We searched through all the markets and didn't see a single piece of the old jewelry, only new tourist junk. Whatever was once old here seemed to have been replaced with all-new cement buildings, a small marketplace, and newly planted date palms surrounding the plaza. We wandered into a small store without a door and noticed some tribal women's clothing hanging on the wall. No one came to help us, but this was what Morocco was like without guides.

As we were looking around, suddenly a man appeared who started screaming and then pulled a dagger out from under his djellaba. He had no interest in us but seemed to be looking for the owner, who came out from a back room and drew his own knife. Both were now dancing around each other, wielding their knives, while we found ourselves in their way. Linda and I began sliding along the adobe walls until we reached the open entrance. We heard some muffled sounds as we ran toward our rental car. So much for Tiznit.

We were now on our way to Goulimine, famous for its ceramic trade beads, on the edge of the Western Sahara Desert. It is a walled town with houses built out of sun-dried red clay, and at the time was encircled by sand dunes. Originally made in Venice, the trade beads were called *millefiori* and used as currency in Sub-Saharan Africa, especially during the slave trade. We wanted to see what we might find there.

Outside of town we attracted a professional-type tourist guide riding a motorcycle who was trying to talk to me through the window of the rental car as we were both traveling about thirty-five miles an hour. He shouted at me, "My brother, please stop. Let me show you the nomads of the desert." He was so persistent he convinced us to follow him to a nearby oasis. We went a few kilometers more to the lush oasis with an old elongated adobe building and a few black tents surrounding the water well. We noticed another rental car, a Renault, on the trail leading to the adobe buildings. Our new friend on the motorcycle invited us into one of the rooms and served us tea. He was eager to learn more about us and life in America, practice his English, and tell us about his friend who now lived in Detroit.

I heard a motor running and I knew it must be the Renault that was on the trail and now leaving. We were then escorted into the next building, an elongated adobe structure with only a few windows, which felt damp even though we were on the edge of the Sahara.

In the room where we were taken, two men wearing dark blue indigo robes with face scarves hiding half their faces were sitting together on leather mats. These men were Tuaregs, the so-called raiders and outlaws of the Sahara, yet the best silversmiths and leatherworkers in Africa, who also looked striking with their high cheekbones and chiseled features.

The men said hello, welcomed us, ordered tea, and then began to show us their wares for sale. They were junk—the worst of the worst tourist jewelry from Marrakech. We sat for a while, trying to be polite, but then I got frustrated as I kept asking them to show me their good stuff and they continued to shove cheap glass bead necklaces our way. I finally stood up and opened a nearby trunk, and inside was a treasure trove: silver necklaces, earrings, and bracelets with inlaid ebony wood and elaborate hand stamping. It was a true education for us to see this variety of jewelry from the south that we had never seen in Marrakech. I glanced at Linda, who was smiling at me, and then I negotiated. Everyone was left happy, and we had an outstanding collection of jewelry, the one thing we had come looking for.

Once our business was finished, motorcycle man told us that one of his family members had a lot of the leather Tuareg items for sale: elaborately dyed and tooled camel bags that women and men stored their precious belongings in as they traveled nomadically, and larger ones that they used to bring salt from the Sahara Desert for trade. He drove ahead of us to another low adobe building. Linda and I entered and realized that everyone there had taken off their shoes, so we knew we needed to do that also. We sat inside a room with low banquettes and stuffed cushions. A man came in, introduced himself as Aziz, and began showing us leather camel cushions and window trappings. Most of them had a thin layer of mold, and some had a serious amount of gray mildew. I started complaining that he was wasting our time with all this junk. Aziz, seeing how upset I was, said he had better stuff in another fonduk and asked us to wait and he would bring it to us. Aziz's scam, which we figured out, was that he didn't have any other pieces tucked away somewhere waiting for a paying customer. Instead he was running all over town, looking for good pieces from his friends and relatives to show us.

We weren't happy that he had only shown us junk, and now we had to wait. However, we were looking for these kinds of leather items and so far he was the only one we knew who could locate them. We waited for what felt like hours, until finally Linda and I decided to leave. We walked to the foyer, where we had left our shoes, and I discovered that our clever Aziz had taken my shoes on his hunt for the new items, so it seemed impossible for us to leave. I couldn't leave barefoot, but I spotted a pair of leather sandals on the mat that were probably Aziz's, and took those.

We left the house and walked to the center of town. Linda and I shared a laugh as I stumbled in these unfamiliar shoes, which were far too big for me. Finding a small café, we decided to have some tea and wait, knowing Aziz would show up eventually since our Toyota SUV was still at his house. He arrived as we were drinking our second glass of mint tea. He had located a few leather camel bags and other items we were pleased with and bought. He also showed us something we had never before seen or even imagined. These leather pieces were square shaped with a wraparound design and incised with a traditional design. Aziz explained that they were shoes for camels. When the desert sands get too hot, they put these around the hooves so the camels can continue to travel. After all our buying was done, Aziz handed my own shoes back, and he smiled when I told him how clever he had been.

When Linda and I had driven into Goulimine, we noticed an advertisement for a hotel a few kilometers away. So we decided now to find it and stay there overnight. Once we pulled into the parking lot, we recognized the same Renault that was on the road to the Tuareg campground. We met the other travelers later that day and learned how enthusiastic they were about meeting the nomadic Tuaregs in their black tents. We didn't want to disappoint them, but we told them our story about finding the jewelry-filled trunks. They were good natured when they understood they had been scammed, but that attitude also could have been influenced by what they carried with them.

The husband was a liquor salesman from France, and the whole trunk of their car was filled with booze. When we first began talking it was clear they had a buzz on, and it only intensified as the night wore on. Since the four of us were the only guests of the hotel, the small restaurant served us only dates and watery garbanzo soup. The one waiter was so taken with our Walkman and tape of Michael Jackson that we ended up trading it for an antique brass tray. It was a fun, boisterous night, though the next morning we paid the price.

We dragged ourselves into the rental car with a loaf a stale bread and one orange between us and headed farther inland to the town of Tafraout. Hôtel Les Amandiers was the only hotel there, and it resembled a Kasbah with high walls and small, narrow windows. We soon realized we were the only guests in this sixty-room hotel. The town was famous for its shoemakers, and we decided to once again expand our Nomads line with their exquisite hand-embroidered shoes with Goodyear tire-tread soles.

Every day while we were there, Linda and I would visit the shoemakers, walking from the hotel and gazing at the beautiful red-granite mountains that surrounded the city, and had them show us what they had made that day. Even though we had ordered one-hundred pairs of shoes, large, medium, and small, we ended up with eighty pairs of small—another learning experience for us. The difference in price between the leather, the dye, and the embroidery between the large and small size meant they could perhaps make only another fifty cents or so. We eventually sold them to a business person who was taking them to Japan, where most women wore a size five.

The local people were mainly shoemakers, and most of the other businesses in Tafraout revolved around water. We saw water cans of aluminum, brass, or copper in various sizes at most of the shops. We watched as sand-colored Land Rovers, with wider-than-average tires, roared into town with the dust billowing behind them. The drivers, Saharians, seemed to barely notice us as they went about their business buying supplies at this outpost before returning to the desert. Linda insisted on taking a photograph of the sign on the edge of town that said, "52 Jours à Timbuktu," which translated from French meant fifty-two days' journey to Timbuktu.

There wasn't much to eat or do in Tafraout. For dinner we were served canned sardines, eggs, round Hobbs bread, and Henry's cookies. The cookies were wrapped in a red aluminum foil, and we would find them in the most obscure places, making us wonder what kind of preservatives they had. But we made the best of it. We would lounge by the pool in the late afternoon and make love late into the night.

With the one-hundred pairs of shoes shoved in the back of the SUV, and some water containers, we headed toward Taroudant, east of Agadir, and the famous La Gazelle d'Or Hôtel. It became well-known after Winston Churchill stayed there, presumably to go white-wing dove hunting. The grounds included nearly 250 acres, of beautifully landscaped gardens and thirty private bungalows. For the guests it had a stable of Arabian horses, tennis courts, swimming pools, and all else you could imagine.

I had recently been issued an American Express Gold Card and was eager to use it. We arrived after lunch and the hotel appeared deserted. We rang the bell and waited for what seemed like hours before a sleepy-eyed man appeared behind the desk. He asked if I had a reservation, and I told him no. He said, "You came all this way without a reservation?" I replied, "Yes, but I do have an American Express Gold Card." I pushed the card toward him along the counter. He took one long look at me, flicked it back, and said, "One night only."

The hotel guests were stuffy; they all seemed to be old and British. We were informed to be at the restaurant around sunset for cocktail hour and then dinner. I would need to wear a coat and tie, but they would supply them if I didn't have either one. I didn't, and I felt sorry for Linda as she was doing her best to dress up for dinner, but all she had to wear was a pair of black jeans and a silk shirt. We arrived in the salon, where all the guests appeared to be drinking gin and tonics, so we did the same. No one spoke to us, and Linda was the youngest person there by about thirty years. They ushered us into the dining room, and the menu was only in French. We picked something that we thought was meat, and Linda tried to order it medium well, but the snooty waiter said to her in perfect English, "Madame, that is fish." After dinner, we returned to our bungalow and had another romantic evening with the air conditioning at full speed.

The next morning, after being served freshly squeezed juices, croissants, and coffee on trays in bed, we slowly left our beautiful setting and got back on the road toward Marrakech. Forty miles outside of Taroudant I noticed three large antique terracotta olive oil urns on the side of the road with no one visibly around. I stopped and inspected the urns, and before long a young man appeared from nowhere. He spoke only Berber, so I got out my pieces of paper and a pen and started writing down some numbers showing what I was willing to pay for the urns. He shook his head and motioned to me that he wanted clothing, not money. I presumed he didn't value the urns but did value the warm clothes I had on. I pulled out the bag of clothing I had planned to give away, and then the bargaining didn't take long. I had just enough room in the Toyota to jam the three urns in the back seat, surrounded by the tiny shoes.

We continued on to Marrakech, and the sky was now turning black. A storm was approaching, and when we reached the top of the tree line, it began to snow. We rounded a tight corner and noticed

that the gendarmerie (the king's police) were in the process of closing the highway. They questioned us about where we were going, and
we said, "Bab Dukala." "You are the last ones to pass. Drive slowly,"
and they put the chain across the road behind us. We slipped and
slid, hitting a few guard rails even though we were in the SUV. As we
drove slowly down to lower elevations, the snow turned to rain and
continued to rain hard all the way back to Marrakech.

Arriving before dark, we went first to the Bab Dukala warehouse,
and then I searched for Rashid, one of the men who worked for
Parisian, to help me unpack the shoes and pottery from the car. I
found him around the corner painting an outside wall of a home in
the pouring rain. The white paint was running between his legs down
the street, and when I pointed to it and asked him, "Don't you see
that all the paint is washing away?" He said, "Yes, but I was told to
paint the wall this afternoon." Often what you would normally take
for granted never turned out that way in Morocco.

❦ Chapter Eleven ❦

Down and Dirty

◇◇◇◇◇◇◇◇◇◇◇◇◇◇◇◇◇◇◇◇◇◇◇◇◇◇◇◇◇◇◇◇◇◇◇◇◇

LINDA AND I talked about moving out of the CTM Hotel. The owner of the CTM had approached us, not Omar the manager, and said we needed to begin paying more money for the water we were using to wash our rugs. Omar later apologized for it but said his hands were tied. The owner had two young daughters who lived on the top floor of the hotel, and every time we saw them they were eating old paint chips off the adobe walls like candy. It was time to leave Brecka, La Hassan, Omar, and all the morning waiters at the Café de France. I wouldn't miss the one-armed beggar woman, but a few of the shoeshine men I would always remember. The hotel was noisy every morning with the criers calling for clients for the buses, and yet the biggest disadvantage was that it didn't have a restaurant. So often we would return exhausted from the night market at the souks and then had to walk to the Iceberg restaurant or the stalls on the Djemma el Fna to eat.

A new hotel, the Islan, had recently opened across from the Koutoubia Mosque on Mohammed V. The big advantage of the new hotel was the rooftop restaurant. We moved there and were very happy in our new room. It not only had a new air conditioner but also water throughout the day and a window that opened looking out over the Koutoubia Mosque. Watching Linda walk barefoot across the cool tile, with the mosque lit up in the background shining through the window, I knew I was in love.

The hotel's favorite music was a CD of Dean Martin. We knew it by heart. "When the moon hits your eye like a big pizza pie, that's amore. When the world seems to shine like you've had too much wine, that's amore." They played it over and over. The chef used to invite me into the kitchen every night so I could see what the specials were. Not much variety—lemon chicken, kebobs, sole, omelets with baby shrimp. He would occasionally bring me cooked *loubia* beans, Navy beans, from his own home since he knew I liked them.

The owner, manager, chef, and front desk man at the Islan all made our life so easy. Once we walked out the doors and picked up our bicycles, we would get right back into the chaos of Marrakech, but the Islan Hotel became our little respite from it all. In the evening we would sit at the rooftop tables either writing our postcards, doing our numbers, or preparing our radio ads.

By then we had expanded our store in Santa Fe. We started with 1600 square feet and doubled it to 3200—a large store for a small

David Marlow, Photographer

town. One day the host of a local radio program that we liked came into Nomads and suggested we do some radio ads. We'd never done anything like that before and thought, why not? We wrote all our own ads as anecdotes coming from Morocco and used the tagline "From the magical markets of Marrakech." Every month Linda and I would go to the radio station and record our ads. The Islan Hotel was an ideal environment to write them. High above the sidewalks, directly across the street from the mosque, this rooftop viewpoint gave us an exceptional opportunity to observe the people on the street.

One of our favorites was "The desert wind blows hot and dry even into the markets of Marrakech. Everyone around me wears a cotton caftan, and they look so comfortable I trade in my Levi's and never look back. Still going native after all these years, from the magical markets of Marrakech, Nomads brings to you." Another one was "Each night I walk through the Square of the Dead in Marrakech, and the snake charmer calls to me. 'Take me to America,' he cries out. 'Sell me your baskets,' I reply. When morning comes, I wake and find a pile of baskets inside my gate. From the magical markets of Marrakech, the latest collection of treasures at Nomads."

Ever since learning about Brecka wanting a postcard more than anything else, Linda and I had gotten into the habit of sending postcards to our friends in Morocco. Whenever we went anywhere, from Dallas to Minnesota, we would buy ten to twenty postcards and send them off to Marrakech. A few of our friends began putting our postcards on the walls of their small shops.

Realizing how much everyone liked this, we started doing the same thing for our customers in Santa Fe. We discovered a young street urchin postcard seller we liked named Aziz, and every time we arrived in Morocco, we searched him out or asked someone to tell him we were back. Each time we had him bring us one-hundred postcards. Linda and I would write postcards at night until our fingers cramped. I always said the same thing "La bes, really hot here, lots of flies, but still finding great treasures." Linda would write a lot more, but we both ended with "Thank you for your interest in Nomads." Years later a woman came into our store and told us her mother had just died. As she was going through her things, she found a packet of postcards from us that her mother had saved. It was worth the sore fingers.

Occasionally Linda and Parisian would have long-drawn-out arguments about how this business was supposed to be run. Linda believed that if she controlled the money, she should get what she wanted, an attitude she had learned from her father. Parisian, on the other hand, believed he could do as he wished if he just said "Enshalah" after every promise.

One day Linda and Parisian got into a fierce argument that lasted all morning. We had received many handbag orders from the most recent Dallas gift show. Although Parisian loved to make the kilim purses, he didn't enjoy dealing with the old men who made the hand-braided dagger straps. There were still only three old men who knew how to do this braiding, and Parisian had gotten tired of dealing with them and their slow-paced work. So when we arrived back in Marrakech, he had one-hundred handbags ready for us—with no straps.

I could hear them from the rooftop terrace of the warehouse, where I was washing rugs. I finally stopped and descended the narrow staircase, which was always dangerous to walk down, especially at night. Parisian saw me and immediately ceased arguing. He had a great deal of respect for me, but my wife was another matter. *"Jebu toot sweet"*—"Come with me quickly"—"Parisian," I said, and he followed me through the oversized studded door to the small alley outside.

I reached into my pocket, took out a new, crisp hundred-dollar bill, and asked him, "Will you just shut up and quit arguing?"

"For a hundred dollars," he replied, "I will do anything you request."

"Then please be quiet with my wife and get her the straps."

"OK, OK, *sabess maken*"—"no problem"—and then he asked the question he had always wanted to know: "Does she treat you like this in America?"

"Only sometimes, Enshalah," I replied.

The next morning Parisian showed up with some fresh croissants, and Linda, who was still angry because we hadn't gotten the handbag straps, avoided him and went to the rooftop. Perhaps because of the argument the day before, he began speaking to me about his wife, a subject that rarely came up. Parisian had gotten married late in life and wanted to have children. His mother had chosen a woman to be his wife; he had no say in the matter. Supposedly she had gone to small villages nearby, knocked on doors, and asked if there were any virgins there. He told me that the marriage was difficult because his wife was so unhappy.

"I don't understand why," he said. "She has two djellabas. What more does she want?"

"Well, if you and your wife are so unhappy, why don't we just pay her father to take her back?"

"I will have to wait until my boys get older, or they will hold me responsible."

I walked away thinking how different marriage life was in the States and Morocco. A few months later I was back in Marrakech, this time alone.

One day I decided to go to Bab el Khemis, a huge outdoor flea market like a mini version of the Rose Bowl flea market in Pasadena. I had heard that everything old or used in the Moroccan world was for sale there. Though it was open every day, the best day was Thursday, or before prayers on Friday.

At daybreak on Thursday, as the prayers began to end and the sun was rising, I headed to the market on my bicycle. I hoped I was going in the right direction. It was somewhere across town through the medina in an area I was not familiar with. I just followed the people with donkey carts loaded with used treasures and became part of the caravan.

In the alleys of Marrakech you always needed to be alert. I came across a large group of people gathering in a small alley near the bus station. The crowd, all young men and small boys, was continuing to grow by the second as I rode up. I was curious, so I parked my bicycle and wormed my way into the inner circle. I observed two men pushing each other and yelling. One of the men stopped pushing, took off his shirt, showing his muscular, tattooed chest, and then ripped his leather belt with a big buckle off his pants and began swinging it around and hitting the other man. The crowd went wild, seeing blood, and egged the tattooed man on.

His opponent was standing still and taking all the blows. I thought he must either be mentally impaired or far-sighted and couldn't see the belt coming at him. Within minutes he had numerous welts on his back and was bleeding out of his right ear. Witnessing this I couldn't take it anymore. I took a roll of coins out of my pocket that

I had received the day before from the bank, intending to give them to the beggars that followed me. With the coins in my right hand, I waited for the tattooed man to make his advance.

"*Ash biti*"—"what do you want?"—he said to me as I moved to stand between the two of them.

"You tell me," I said, and he came at me swinging the belt. I ducked under it and punched him in the solar plexus with the fist holding the coins, which made my punch more powerful. He went down coughing and holding his rib cage. The crowd now changed who they favored and started kicking and pickpocketing the bully on the ground. I knew the authorities would be coming soon, so I sneaked back through the crowd because the police were certain to arrest all the people who were watching, whether they were involved or not.

It turned out that the muscular, tattooed man was from Tangiers and had ties to the hashish business. The man's friends came looking for me a few days later, but since I wasn't from that part of the medina, no one knew me, so what had happened was soon forgotten—except in the Berber rug market, where the walls had ears. Word finally spread there about what had happened on my way to the flea market, and how I had helped the bully's opponent. The people in the rug market looked me in the eyes and said they wished they could have helped.

After the fight I continued about a quarter mile through a wide, crowded alley and approached what I believed to be Bab el Khemis. In an area the size of an American football field were vendors, buyers, beggars, and fortune-tellers all huddled on blankets or carpets, or squatting in the dirt. It was similar to Djemma el Fna because the crowd was so colorful and interesting with all the faces from different parts of Morocco. I also heard the braying of a multitude of donkeys, all seemingly talking to each other at the same time. I always thought the donkeys loved the markets the most because they missed their friends and looked forward to seeing each other every Thursday.

It was here that I found myself alone, the only foreigner among the townspeople and the mountain tribesmen. For some reason I was not afraid and started wandering, head down, not making eye contact until I suddenly noticed I was surrounded by a group of angry flea market buyers. They seemed to be focusing their anger on me, and I didn't know what I had done to attract so much attention. Everyone was shouting and pushing to see what was happening. Unexpectedly I was pushed to the ground and felt dirty fingers and greedy hands going through my pockets. I felt like I was glued to the ground and would be smothered by all the moving bodies. Gasping for air, I started shouting, "Salaam Alaikum! Salaam Alaikum!"—"Peace be unto you!"

Out of nowhere, as if God were protecting me, came Said, a giant man from the Berber market who I had gifted previously with a clock for his home. Said started pulling and tugging the people off me like he was Hercules and then lectured the mob about how good a person I was and that God had brought me to Marrakech. Immediately the crowd backed off, and everyone said, "Merhabban."

I had met Said years before when I was looking for the biggest men in Marrakech to help me in the market when it got a little hectic. Not everyone liked me, and they would sometimes spit on the ground and say, "The devil is here," or unnecessarily push or shove me from behind.

So when I spied Said working in the rug auction, I was lucky. He was a Berber man with a childlike disposition from a small town in the High Atlas Mountains. He couldn't hear well and had trouble conversing. I presumed he couldn't read or write, and many people made fun of him since he was always dressed in rags.

I asked Said one day if there was anything in the world that he wanted, and he said, "I would like a wind-up clock. I live in the countryside with no electricity, and I cannot be late for work."

Haj Ben Sherriff had seen me speaking to Said and asked, "What does that poor man want from you?"

"Just a wind-up clock for his home."

Haj looked at me and said, "I need one too."

On my next trip to Marrakech I brought two clocks: one for the poorest man and the other for the richest.

I'd been in Morocco enough times to have observed a couple of the scams that the street kids and young men committed around the

Djemma el Fna. One of the most common often occurred around a small restaurant near Café du Progrès called Snack Hippies. Snack Hippies was famous for their kafta burgers, which they served on long French bread. It was a hangout for many young European and some American travelers who were attracted to the name. I would see many of them hanging there, attempting to buy a little hashish from the few Moroccans that sold it. A young Moroccan man would approach them and whisper in their ear, "Spices for the mind, my friend?" If the hippies wanted some, which most of them did, the Moroccan man would ask for the money and say he would return in a few minutes. Soon he would rush back and say with alarm that they had just been observed by the secret police and that they should run for their lives. Not knowing what to expect, they did run and never went back to Snack Hippies. This went on all the time and was one of the many scams around the square.

Smoking a little hashish in Morocco seemed natural, but the secret was to buy just a pinch from as few people as possible. I had never considered dealing drugs or becoming a trafficker—for several reasons. I had been to Istanbul and the Pudding Shop about the same time the movie *Midnight Express* was filmed. Going to prison in Morocco terrified me, even though I knew I would be able to survive it. But it would have cost me weekly since in Morocco it is your family or loved ones that pay to keep you alive. If I had been sent to prison in the States, it would have been a disgrace to my family. I decided early on that even though I knew there was a lot of money to be made, I would stick with the rugs. The rugs were better than the drugs, just without the D.

Another scam was only attempted after you had become acquainted with the Moroccan a little bit. They handed you a note written in terrible English asking for money because one of their family members had been arrested. The note always said to please keep it a secret.

I also learned about tipping, or bribes, which I saw as a necessary art form. With time I became an expert, but in the beginning it was a trial-and-error learning experience. I would travel with my safari jacket with multiple pockets and different amounts in each pocket. I would size up the situation, looking for the person who seemed to be in control or who had the most stripes on his shoulders. I would approach him with confidence, introduce myself, and ask his name. I would then inquire if he was married and had a family. I would be sympathetic and comment on how expensive it must be to have a large family. I would think of a number, times it by two, and know which of my pockets to pick from. As I shook his hand I would say, "This is for your wife and children."

⚘ Chapter Twelve ⚘

Walking in
Different Shoes

◇◇◇◇◇◇◇◇◇◇◇◇◇◇◇◇◇◇◇◇◇◇◇◇◇◇◇◇◇◇◇◇

Abdul 1 and I continue to be good friends, and I would always hire him when I came to town. My other business friends never liked Abdul, they just tolerated him, but he was unique in that he never went back to them and asked for any commission. He had dropped out of school at a young age to help his family, and he lived on Riad Zitone just down the alley from the Café du Progrès.

He lived there with his mother and a beautiful sister who looked like a young Sophia Loren. Her name was Miriam, and she was always there when I would be invited for lunch. At my first lunches I would just hear her footsteps on the stairs, but after numerous meals she would help her mother serve the tagine, and smile at me with an occasional wink. Abdul frequently told me that his sister liked me, and I noticed I was never invited to his home for lunch when Linda was in town.

A few days after my experience at the Bab el Khemis flea market, Muammar Gaddafi, the prime minister of Libya, was expected to come to Marrakech for a meeting of all the North African countries. The king of Morocco had been on television to tell the people to come out and line the streets to celebrate Gaddafi's visit. The king also told them to wear their best djellabas so it would be a grand showing of support. The Marrakech people put their best djellabas not on themselves but rather on wooden cross-like frames and thrust them about in the air like political posters outside a polling area.

It was on this afternoon, as I was waiting for the king and Gaddafi's entourage, that someone stepped on my foot—and held it there. The person who had her foot on mine was a young woman dressed totally covered except for her eyes. The more I looked at her—she still had not removed her foot from mine—the more I began to recognize her as Abdul's sister, Miriam.

I had been told that if a woman stepped on your foot and kept it there, this was a sign that she was a prostitute. She would step on a possible customer's foot to indicate her profession without creating any suspicion from those around them. I pretended not to know her and walked a little farther away, waiting for the parade to be over. After that incident Miriam never assisted her mother at the lunches anymore, and I never told Abdul.

A few weeks later Linda joined me and wanted to go to the Dar Yacout Restaurant she had just read about in a travel magazine. The Yacout was the first of now many Moroccan cuisine restaurants in very old villas in the medina that had been renovated.

The night of the dinner Linda dressed up in one of Boujma's finest Egyptian cotton caftans and put on an expensive amber and coral necklace we had bought that day from Yousef for Nomads. We hailed a taxi, and after saying, "Peacemela," we asked him to take us to the Yacout. The driver had no idea where it was. He drove around in what we thought was the general area, and finally stopped and asked someone on the street. He motioned us to follow him as he walked up about another block, halted, and pointed down an alley, telling us it was there. We were in the middle of the medina, where there were no other foreigners, and he said that we must get out and walk, that the cars can't get through the alley, which was true.

As Linda and I walked down the alley, it continued getting narrower as it twisted and turned. It was dark and scary. We were holding hands, not saying anything out loud, but I suspect both of us were thinking that at any moment someone could come out with a dagger and rob us. We made another turn when a tall Moroccan man with a bright red Fez hat stepped out from the shadows and said, "I believe you are looking for me." He picked up a punched-iron Moroccan lantern and guided us to a wide door that he opened for us. Rose petals were scattered all over the floor as he led us to the rooftop terrace. The terrace view overlooked the medina, with the Koutoubia Mosque visible in the distance.

Musicians with Gnowee guitars sat on the floor of the terrace playing for us as we were served our first cocktail and almonds. After an hour we descended the stairs to a private room overlooking a small pool to the first of many courses of fabulous food: Moroccan tagines, couscous, salads, lemon chicken, and all the red wine you could drink.

When we were ready to leave, we stood outside the restaurant with the doorman, waiting for a taxi. There was a street, in the opposite direction from the route we had taken, where we would be able to see taxis driving nearby. We finally saw one in the distance, and the doorman whistled and then blocked the street, stopping the driver and telling the Moroccan customers sitting in the back seat to get out so we could get in. He told the driver to come back and get them. We gave the doorman a generous tip and went off into the night. This was yet another side to Morocco.

The next day we took some friends from the States shopping and went to Klayna's store. He always had a lot of souvenirs, and Linda and I enjoyed talking with him while they looked around. We had seen a poster with his picture on it, plastered on the wall in beggar's alley, so we asked him about it. Klayna told us he was running for a city councilman seat in his neighborhood. We had never met anyone else in Marrakech who had any interest in politics. In fact, no one ever discussed anything political because it was a kingdom with a lot of spies. We were impressed with Klayna for wanting to make a difference.

We asked him if he thought he might win, and he said no. We asked why. He explained that the person who was running against him had gone door to door in the neighborhood, asking the residents to vote for him—and what size shoe they wore. He returned a few days later and gave all of them only the right shoe, saying that if he won he would bring them the left shoe. Klayna shook his head sadly and said because of that he didn't stand a chance. Linda and

I were thinking what a sad political situation that was, and then remembered our own U.S. history when politicians would give out half pints of whiskey near the polling places.

I had started traveling with six large duffle bags whenever I went to Morocco so I could carry more merchandise back to the States. I would get two bags checked for free and pay the additional fifty dollars at the airport for one more. To manage the remaining three, I would arrive at the Casablanca airport early, long before my plane was to leave, and look for American tourists who were traveling to New York. If I noticed people who were only going to check one bag, I asked them if they would help me and check one of my bags with theirs, and then gave them one of the beautiful handwoven grain baskets that I carried with me. This always seemed to work, and the airline got used to me doing this. Once I landed in JFK I would claim all six bags and hire a porter to get me through customs and on to the next terminal.

Several other businessmen were on these flights from Casablanca to JFK, and we recognized each other. We never talked between us, each protecting his own ideas or the treasures he was finding. One such gentleman, a tall, wiry figure with deep-set eyes and a large nose, always wore a suit and tie. That was odd because it was the era of the "leisure suits," supposedly to make it appear like you were on the way to the gym. I always loved the safari adventurer look, so I would wear khaki pants and shirts with many pockets and shoulder epaulets.

One hot afternoon the man in the suit arrived at the Casa airport the same time I showed up with my six duffle bags. He came over to me and asked, "Why do you travel with so much luggage?" I responded that my business was antique textiles from Morocco, but I purposely didn't mention the handbag business. He then opened his suit jacket and displayed rows of gold Fatima hands, all neatly safety-pinned in place. He said he sold them to the Jewish and Arab merchants in New York, and smiling widely he walked to the ticket counter and said, "No weight."

Linda and I had now outgrown the Islan Hotel, and Parisian had found us another home in Bab Dukala before one of our return trips to Marrakech. The taxi drove us directly to the old home that my friend had rented in the medina. The home had eight orange trees and two date palms growing in the middle of the courtyard. Cluttered with oranges on the ground, it looked like no one had lived there for years. There was a nook built into the thick tile wall by the front door for a guard to sleep, and for a few years men would knock on our door wanting that job. The home had two floors and a rooftop terrace perfect for washing and drying rugs. Parisian had supplied us with beds, sheets, towels, and one bar of soap. The kitchen had only a dirt floor and chains with cuffs on their wall, where I suspected the original owners had kept their slaves. The shower floor was so cold we placed a wood pallet on it to make it easier to stand on as the lukewarm water washed over us.

Even though Linda and I were exhausted from the trip, we had a difficult time sleeping that first night in Bab Dukala. The home was more than three hundred years old, and we both felt that spirits were there. The bedroom opened on the garden, so the smell of the oranges was wonderful, but getting up to go to the toilet at night was spooky, and it took some getting used to. The alley cats walked the rooftops at night, and even though the streets were much quieter than sleeping at the CTM on the square, we heard noises most of the night.

It was all worth it, though, since we were able to buy our own food and cook meals at home. One of our memorable stories was buying a chicken to barbeque. The butchers had only live chickens in cages, so we picked the one we wanted and then asked the butcher to pluck the feathers after he killed it. Not a problem, it was something he did every day. But then we asked him to cut it into pieces for us. He looked confused yet laid the whole chicken on the cutting board and cut it from head to tail in quarter pieces. No breast, thigh, neck, gizzards, anything, just whack, whack, into equal sizes. Each of the pieces included a section of breast, part of a wing, perhaps a thigh section, whatever.

One day Linda and I went up to the rooftop to see the Atlas Mountains and the sunset. One neighbor trained homing pigeons and would often be there right at sunset. It was entertaining to watch. A smaller half-roof area gave us a higher ceiling in the main downstairs room, and we climbed a ladder to that area for a better view.

We heard a loud noise and happened to look down and saw women running to hide. They were our neighbors, and we had unintentionally looked down into their riad, which was forbidden. The medina people all live so close together that they respect each other's privacy and never look down from the rooftops into their neighbors' homes. We quickly got down, knowing they had seen us too, and that night we heard a lot of noise on the roof. The next morning we went up to our terrace, and our rooftop was littered with broken glass. In Morocco, seeing women in their homes uninvited was a serious mistake. We had never met these neighbors, nor any of our other neighbors in Bab Dukala, and not everyone liked our being there.

Linda had been to enough lunches and had seen enough kitchens by now to have realized that one thing the women never had was any kind of oven mitt or kitchen towels. So she had gotten into the habit of bringing over several sets to use as gifts. We decided to take one of them, wrap it in tissue paper and ribbon, and throw it over the wall into our neighbor's courtyard. The next morning we went up to our terrace, where we had swept up all the broken glass, and found a dozen red roses that had been thrown over our wall.

While we were still in Marrakech, we decided to try to get a booth at the Los Angeles gift show so we could exhibit our merchandise there. Leon and his mother would continue do the shows for us in Dallas while we expanded into California. The Los Angeles show had 80,000 buyers registered, and at the time was the second-largest merchandise show in the U.S.

Back in the States I filled out the application to exhibit and sent in some pictures of the items we wished to show. I received a letter back saying all the booths were already taken, and we were on a waiting list. The advertising people for the show catalog didn't know this and called me a few days later asking if we would be interested in placing an ad. My years in Morocco had trained me by then, so I said, "I would love to place a full-page color ad in your catalog, but unfortunately I don't have a booth and am on a waiting list." The woman paused for a moment and then said she would call us back. By the end of the day we had a booth.

We then began working on what we would bring. We already knew the handbag business would be easy, but we also wanted to show our one-of-a-kinds.

The show opened at ten a.m. Saturday morning, and we were totally unprepared. We sold out the first day, and for the next two days we sat in an empty booth with only our handbag samples. The first night we thought it was so great, and how cool we were, to be in a business that was so happening. The second day we realized how stupid we were not to have brought more merchandise.

We continued to exhibit at the twice-yearly show for the next ten years. After a few shows the management relocated us to the front row because of the uniqueness of our merchandise. I loved the action of the shows and the unlimited possibilities. I began to feel it was my duty to continue to find new and interesting items for all the stores that bought from us. We designed painted side tables and night-stands, jewelry boxes, bread boxes, mirror frames, all hand-painted and made in Morocco. We took old water jug pottery and turned them into table lamps. We also created an office supply line. We even tried an inlaid bone mortuary box for people's ashes—our only big failure—though we eventually sold them all by changing the name to treasure chest.

One afternoon during our last L.A. show, I glanced around and realized that most of my best clients were getting older and closing their shops or planning to. And not many young people were getting into the business. In our last few shows we experienced some competition, whereas for years we were the only ones importing from Morocco. With additional booths displaying imports from there, the items were becoming more familiar and no longer unique. Linda and I discussed it and decided it was time to get out.

Chapter Thirteen

Finding the Gold

ⵯⵯⵯ

ONE NIGHT about six weeks later in Marrakech I was sitting alone on the rooftop terrace facing the mountains. I closed my eyes for a few moments and asked my senses to take over.

I began to pick up the scent of olives and olive oil, and it only became stronger the longer I kept my eyes closed. I then questioned myself on why I hadn't considered this business before. One reason was obvious—I didn't really like olives and knew nothing about the oil. I sat there well after dark that evening, thinking about these products. The next morning I went looking for answers to my new questions.

I had always seen Boujma 2 drinking olive oil for breakfast, which he would occasionally offer me, but the idea of swallowing it made me sick. That morning I went in search of Boujma and found him at his usual place having breakfast with a few friends. They were all sitting around on carpets, sipping tea, and eating bread with olive oil. They again asked if I wanted to join them, and this time I accepted their offer. It was not what I expected. Thus began my next adventure—the olive oil business.

Through research I discovered that Morocco was the second-largest supplier of olives and olive oil in the world. The majority of their products was consumed by Moroccans, and the rest was shipped to waiting buyers in Spain and Italy, where it was then bottled and sold as being from those countries. Why had we all thought that Italy was the best and main supplier? This was an intriguing business because it was veiled in mystery and lies.

Boujma promised me he would go to his family village and get me a bottle of the fresh-pressed olive oil he wanted me to taste. He got word to me in a few days that he had the oil and to join him for lunch. After a large meal of lemon chicken and couscous with vegetables, with several of his relatives attending, he opened a used water bottle and poured out a portion of olive oil into a white bowl. This oil did not look like what I was used to seeing in the stores in the States. It was dark green, cloudy, and smelled exactly like apple cider. It was a fruit not a vegetable oil. This was the real McCoy. My only question to myself was, is America ready for something so different from what they have been buying?

After lunch I quickly went to find Haj Midi because I knew he had olive groves on his farm outside of Marrakech. I told him about my new plan of getting into the olive oil business. He didn't seem surprised but just asked why it had taken me so long to find the real gold in his country.

With the sample Boujma had given me, I started to hunt for a supplier and a shipper with a license to ship food, which was different from the artisanal shipping license we already had. Parisian and I spent nearly a week riding on his motorcycle, looking for someone to help us. I found lots of olive oil but none with the quality I now knew existed. Starting to give up hope, we followed a large truck loaded with olives into the industrial quarter. It parked outside a factory for only a few minutes before someone opened the gates and let the truck in. I squeezed in just before the gate closed but was greeted by the guard. I used my standard method of "tipping," and he motioned me to follow him through the factory to the offices.

I waited in a room for at least twenty minutes before a young man dressed in a white laboratory jacket entered and greeted me. He first spoke to me in Arabic, then French, and finally English. While we were speaking English he realized I was an American and introduced himself as Mustapha. He told me he loved the Dallas Cowboys and had gone to a university there. I showed him my olive oil sample and asked if he could produce this quality.

"Where did you get this?" he asked.

"A village outside of Marrakech."

Mustapha then said this was the quality that the old people remember, before the business became so mechanized. "Please come back tomorrow at ten a.m.," he said and ushered me out.

Leaving the building, I found Parisian still sitting on his motorbike. He asked me what happened and I lied, because I knew the system in Morocco would have Parisian coming back for his commission. So I told him they couldn't help me. That evening back on my terrace in Bab Dukala, I celebrated with a few drinks of tequila and tonic, which I had discovered really helped combat food poisoning. I decided to go and eat on the square tonight at the famous stall 36.

By living in Bab Dukala, I avoided having to ride my bike through the medina and could just take the two-lane bypass around it. Stall 36 was not easy to find because it was in the heart of the square surrounded by many other food stalls. The owner specialized in kafta, Moroccan white loubia beans, and lamb cutlets.

The square restaurants had changed since the first year I was there. They were now all food stalls on wheels, lit not by the lanterns as before but with bare light bulbs hung on wires supported by metal poles. Everyone had an extension cord plugged into some outlet somewhere. The old wooden benches were still there, and I always chose a seat close to the stall entrance. When tourists stopped to look at the menu, I told them this was the second-best restaurant stall in the square. This caught their attention and almost always they would ask me where the best one was. I replied that it was a secret and took a few days to find it. Most of the tourists would take my advice and eat at stall 36, so I always got something free on the house.

I arrived at the olive factory a little after ten a.m. by riding my bicycle as recklessly as I could since it was farther than I had realized. The guard was really pleased to see me and led me to Mustapha's office. Dressed again in his white laboratory jacket, Mustapha escorted me to his father's sparsely decorated office. His father didn't speak any English, so Mustapha translated. After the handshake and the motion to please sit, Mustapha listened to his father speaking in Arabic and then said to me, "My father has two questions for you: How did you get into his factory, and the second question, where is your Mercedes and driver?"

I told him that the guard at the entrance was very polite yesterday, so I gave him a little money to help his family. As to the other question, I responded that my bicycle was my Mercedes in Morocco. His father spoke and Mustapha translated again, stating that the guard had been a childhood friend of his father, and that he was pleased I had helped his family. I offered his father a taste of my sample, and then had Mustapha ask him if he would be able to provide this quality of oil for me. After a long discussion between father and son in Arabic, Mustapha finally said to me that they would be able to provide me with thirty drums of this quality, the very first pressing. He then mentioned that I had found the real butter of Marrakech, the *zepta*.

The price had not yet been established because it was early in the season and the prices fluctuate. His father also wanted me to buy his other products. I learned that they had both green and black canned olives, a three-kilo vacuum-pressed bag of salt-cured black olives, and also apricots. I said no to the apricot business but allish-alah—why not?—to the olive products. Suddenly I was immersed in the olive and olive oil business.

We had a few more meetings before I returned to the States. I asked about having the oil bottled and labeled there, but they told me it wasn't possible. Instead it would be shipped in large plastic drums that each held 220 liters.

I returned to Santa Fe thrilled with my new business, and now Linda and I got busy trying to find someone to bottle the oil when it arrived and to design the label. We again planned to use the name Nomads for the oil and collaborated with a Santa Fe designer to incorporate an ancient map of Morocco with a Berber man on an Arabian horse. I knew full well that we had thirty drums of oil arriving and not one customer.

The olive and olive oil business became the next great adventure we had sought. We began exhibiting in Fancy Food shows around the country. This business continued for many years, and the olive oil became a good boost to the Nomads bottom line. Unfortunately, after a few years Mustapha told me that although he liked me, he hated our government and didn't want to supply us anymore. He had become anti-West, and even though his father wanted to continue to

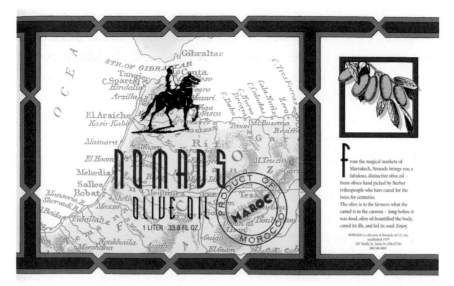

sell to us, Mustapha refused. And he had quit watching the Dallas Cowboys games.

A few months after starting the new business I was back in Marrakech without Linda. I visited the Berber market as usual, but as on other recent trips the rugs of any value to me were absent from the market. In all the years we had been coming to Morocco, fewer and fewer of the antique, tightly woven rugs or capes were coming up for sale. When I questioned Moulay Sherriff about it, he said, "The hands are gone." He explained that most of the older women who used to weave these rugs had died, and the young women were more interested in moving from the mountains to the cities to work for the Coca-Cola factories.

On another late October trip to Morocco I was on the search for a new olive oil source and knew it might be difficult. I had brought a lot of cash over with me, hoping to grease the wheel a little bit. After two weeks I didn't have any success finding a new supplier, but finished my other buying for Nomads and was leaving Morocco from the Casablanca airport.

Inside the airport I broke two of my cardinal rules of travel: never go through customs early, and always mingle with a large group of people. I noticed what looked like a new airport café. I approached a custom agent sitting alone. "La bes." "La bes alec." This custom agent stood up and was at least six-foot-four, with a big bushy mustache, and had dark sunglasses on. He asked for my passport and became interested in all the stamps and visas.

He asked, "Do you have any Moroccan dirhams, euros, or U.S. dollars?"

"Sure, a little," I replied.

"Show me." I pulled out a few dirhams, and then he said, "Any more?" I pulled out a few euros, hoping that the inquiry would end there. Then he demanded, "Do you have any dollars?"

Before I could answer, he said something in Arabic, and another agent entered the room from a side door. Both agents picked me up by my elbows, raising my feet off the floor, and took me to a small office. I wasn't all that nervous because I was well schooled in the Moroccan shakedown.

This office had the mandatory large picture of the king on the wall and nothing else. They ordered me to stand still and raise my hands above my head. Wrapped around my waist were two money belts where I had hidden $20,000 in new one-hundred-dollar bills still wrapped in the bank bands. I had been intending to use it as a deposit for the olive oil crop this year. They pulled out all my money and spread it on the metal table. I could tell the agents were thinking they had caught either a drug dealer or a money launderer. It was too much money for me to say, "Let's share," and too much for them to steal it all without speaking to their supervisors. They asked me no other questions, and one of them picked up the telephone and called someone. While the money lay on the table, it was beginning to dawn on me that I could be in a lot of trouble. "Sit down, *besh-wea*"—"be quiet."

It seemed like a long time before someone came in. A rather handsome, well-dressed Moroccan official entered the small office with a manila folder under his arm. Without asking anything he said, "Thomas Richard Lawrence, take your money and come with me." I gathered up the money, shoving it in every available pocket and followed him out.

Halfway down the hall I knew this could become dangerous; I was all on my own. I began to think I should have bribed the custom agents. We ascended a flight of stairs and entered a long hallway lined with offices occupied by military personnel. At the end of the hall a man stood up from his desk where he guarded the large entrance to another government office. He saluted, and my host gently pushed me through the entrance and walked directly to his desk. He motioned me to sit in one of the overstuffed leather chairs and then said, "Thomas Richard Lawrence, do not think that we do not know you. We have been watching you since you first arrived in 1978. You have been very generous to the people in Marrakech, and the customs officials also. In Casablanca you cannot so easily bribe them as you do in Marrakech."

He then introduced himself as Mohammed Bashir and told me he was head of customs for the whole country. He had inherited the position from his father, who was a close friend of the king's family.

Mohammed asked, "What are you doing with all this money?"

I replied, "I brought the dollars to Morocco to buy olive oil, but there wasn't enough of the good-quality oil because you have a shortage in the country this year."

He realized I was telling the truth. Everyone knew of the shortage of oil, and I was certain that from the information in the manila folder he also knew I had been in the olive oil business now for a few years. He stood up and said, "Let's go have a kawa halib at the VIP lounge. It will give me a chance to practice my English."

Once we were seated in the lounge with our coffees, Mohammed turned toward me to ask a few other questions. "Whatever happened to the microphone and PA system that you brought over for the Iman at the Koutoubia Mosque?" I said, "As far as I know, they are still using it." Mohammed then mentioned that he had been told it had made a huge difference. He then asked me when I would convert and come pray with them. "Enshalah," I replied. He also asked, as had other people in the past, "What has happened to the other good Americans who used to come here for business." I could only respond with "I don't know." Mohammed, a charming conversationalist, had all my documents stamped without my having to stand in any other lines, and also got me an upgrade to business class on Royal Air Maroc. And in case I ever needed him, he gave me his personal cell phone number.

When I returned to Santa Fe and told Linda what had happened, she was furious. She didn't know I had taken that much cash, and when she learned I almost lost it all at the Casablanca airport, not to mention what could have happened on the U.S. side by exceeding the limit of $10,000, she didn't speak to me for a few days. In hindsight it might not have been my best idea.

Klayna once asked me, "Where do I find a woman like Linda, willing to work hard and help me?" I said, "Minnesota," but deep down I knew I was lucky.

Morocco still called to me, and I could not stay away for long—so I planned another trip to Marrakech. Parisian picked me up at the airport as he always did, and I settled back into my home in Bab Dukala.

North Africa was rapidly changing, becoming much more modern, with the Berber tribes moving into the larger cities. The Moroccan king was even talking about allowing more personal freedoms.

I loved Morocco, but I did feel a bit of anger about the business climate; there was always some sort of problem. As a culture, Moroccans bought one cigarette a day, thinking only for the moment since the future was too uncertain, as only God wills it. I told them this was why American business people went to Asia instead of North Africa, but I don't think anyone really understood it.

After the first week I missed Linda, her advice and criticism, and her companionship through the narrow alleys and souks. In all the many times I traveled there, I was never lonely for the first five or six days. The nonstop action of buying enough merchandise to fill forty-foot containers, besides all the luncheons I was always invited to, was self-gratifying. I would hardly eat at all in the evening. I never expected that my success in this business would lead me to live in Marrakech full time, and I was always excited when it was time to leave.

I enjoyed watching the pigeons coming home to roost from my rooftop, and heading into the Berber market looking for treasures and seeing old friends. As I reflected on my rooftop one night, I wondered who would ever have imagined that a surfing excursion would turn into a business and a lifestyle. I had never forgotten what my senses experienced the first time I entered the Square of the Dead. How lucky I was to have been there at the right time and place. Marrakech was my passion. The intrigue, the smells, and the friendships were all my *mekala*—my food. I feasted for many years. I loved it, I lived it, and I'll never forget it.

...more from TR

I wrote *Lawrence of Marrakech*, not only to share the stories of my life in the souks, but with the hope that you may learn some secrets for living, buying and loving life in the casbah. This book is my offering to help you in life.

I am working on my second adventure story about when I imported 12 homes from the jungles of Java, Indonesia and built them on the Pacific coast of Mexico.

Make life an adventure, stay tuned and stay in touch.

 facebook.com/LawrenceofMorocco

 twitter.com/lawrencemorocco

 LawrenceOfMarrakech.com/
private-collection-augmented-reality

 instagram.com/lawrenceofmorocco

www.LawrenceOfMarrakech.com